Making Sense of
Political Ideology

Communication, Media, and Politics

Series Editor
Robert E. Denton, Jr., Virginia Tech

This series features a broad range of work dealing with the role and function of communication in the realm of politics, broadly defined. Including general academic books, monographs, and texts for use in graduate and advanced undergraduate courses, the series will encompass humanistic, critical, historical, and empirical studies in political communication in the United States. Primary subject areas include campaigns and elections, media, and political institutions. *Communication, Media, and Politics* books will be of interest to students, teachers, and scholars of political communication from the disciplines of communication, rhetorical studies, political science, journalism, and political sociology.

Recent Titles in the Series

Forthcoming

Making Sense of Political Ideology

The Power of Language in Democracy

Bernard L. Brock
Mark E. Huglen
James F. Klumpp
Sharon Howell

ROWMAN & LITTLEFIELD PUBLISHERS, INC.
Lanham • Boulder • New York • Toronto • Oxford

ROWMAN & LITTLEFIELD PUBLISHERS, INC.

Published in the United States of America
by Rowman & Littlefield Publishers, Inc.
A wholly owned subsidiary of The Rowman & Littlefield Publishing Group, Inc.
4501 Forbes Boulevard, Suite 200, Lanham, Maryland 20706
www.rowmanlittlefield.com

P.O. Box 317, Oxford OX2 9RU, UK

British Library Cataloguing in Publication Information Available

Library of Congress Cataloging-in-Publication Data

Making sense of political ideology / Bernard L. Brock . . . [et al.].
    p. cm. — (Communication, media, and politics)
    Includes bibliographical references and index.
    ISBN 0-7425-3670-X (cloth : alk. paper) — ISBN 0-7425-3671-8 (pbk. : alk. paper)
    1. Communication in politics—United States. 2. Rhetoric—Political aspects—United
States. 3. United States—Politics and government. I. Brock, Bernard L. II. Series.
JA85.2.U6M37 2005
320.5'0973—dc22

2005009849

Printed in the United States of America

♾™ The paper used in this publication meets the minimum requirements of American
National Standard for Information Sciences—Permanence of Paper for Printed Library
Materials, ANSI/NISO Z39.48-1992.

Contents

Preface

This project was initially inspired by the work of Bernard L. Brock in his dissertation "A Definition of Four Political Positions and a Description of Their Rhetorical Characteristics," written in 1965. The late 1950s and early 1960s were the zenith of the influence of the scientific paradigm that we discuss in chapter 5. The paradigm drove American liberalism's belief that refined knowledge of social affairs had replaced ideology as the source of political decisions. In 1960, Daniel Bell wrote *The End of Ideology*, declaring that traditional political differences based in ideology were eclipsed by the rise of science. Brock thought otherwise, inspired by the work of Richard Weaver. Writing in *Ethics of Rhetoric* in 1962, Weaver argued that an analysis of language usage was a key to understanding political ideology. He described the tendency of conservatives to argue from definition and of liberals to argue from circumstances. Brock correctly associated these ideas with Kenneth Burke's *Grammar of Motives* (probably also a key influence on Weaver). Burke argued similarly that strategic choices of language were a product of underlying philosophy, and as long as people differed in their philosophy, differences of opinion would follow and ideology would be critical.

In the midst of the chaos of the mid-1960s and drawing on these two works and others, Brock argued that ideology was critical to democracy and that the language used to describe our world and advocate action provided a window into deeper structures of thought and politics. Far from being neutral, the language used to convey political ideas reflected differing attitudes toward change and orientations toward the world.

Over the years, this original thinking about language and politics has formed a large part of the conversations we have all had together as we have each tried to sort out our own sense of politics and public action. Those conversations intensified as politics in the United States came full circle in the last two decades of the twentieth century, with ideology seemingly meaning everything and, eventually, in the twenty-first century, seeming to drive the findings of national intelligence in the months before the United States invaded Iraq. The time of hyper-interest in ideology seemed a good time for us to share our conversations. We offer this book as an invitation. Join us in exploring how language helps us meet the challenges inherent in creating democracy in an ever changing world.

1

Ideological Chaos and Political Gridlock

Political Communication in the Early Twenty-first Century

Early in the twenty-first century, the United States is a politically divided nation. We are trapped in political gridlock, lacking a consensus for governmental direction. The dominant metaphor for describing this condition is a nation of red states and blue states, recalling the television image used to portray electoral votes in the 2000 presidential election. This language is startling because it signifies nothing more than the arbitrary selection of colors chosen to illustrate a map of a single moment in the past. The colors convey nothing of the politics, policies, or attitudes toward change held by the voters in each block.[1]

But perhaps we ought not to be surprised by this artificial image. The shallow expression of our divisions is matched by shallowness of our political identities. Those running for political office today, especially below the level of the presidency, seldom embrace the label of their party. Those running for president attempt to characterize themselves as "centrists" in hopes of getting the majority of voters to identify with them. Along any road in an election year, the legions of yard signs display candidate names and slogans, but rarely their political party. One can watch television for many hours before seeing a campaign ad affiliating a candidate with a party.

Beyond the superficial label of *Republican* or *Democrat*, the common labels of *liberal* and *conservative* do little to help predict where an individual will stand on any particular issue. The term *liberal* has become a label broadly out of favor, hurled most frequently as a pejorative at an opponent who runs from the characterization. Although *conservative* may be more broadly embraced, that term also does not fully characterize the mood or political complexities of red America. Those who hurl the pejorative *liberal* or claim conservative standing often vote huge pork-barrel projects, support a president who has driven the deficit to the highest levels in the nation's history, and long for the day when they will have the power to impose their will on American culture. Those who run from the label *liberal* do so in the name of fiscal restraint and the limitation of government power. But in a nation locked in a fifty-fifty parity, with no promise of escape, neither major political party is able to create a consensus necessary to carry out its particular policies.

Today, policy-oriented labels such as *liberal* and *conservative* are disconnected from a coherent ideological framework. They are devoid of historical content and offer little to predict how one group or the other will respond to changing circumstances. This lack of coherence, context, and predictability has a debilitating effect on political decision making. It produces a political discourse that distances citizens from engaging with one another, and it prevents the vibrant debates and discussions essential for a democratic process. Without a political language grounded in historical and consistent principles, citizens cannot fully enact their responsibilities to shape government policies and respond to ever changing conditions. This breakdown in the language of everyday politics has become especially pronounced in the last few decades, as personalities and images, rather than political philosophy or ideology, have become the bases for decision making.

Without coherent, consistent, and contrasting ideologies, political decision making in the United States evolves in unpredictable, erratic ways. Decisions are disconnected from common understandings. People vote on personality, frequently electing political personalities whose policies they reject. The people and government lack any compass to guide the direction of the nation. When the connections among ideology, language, and action break, the viability of the political system gives way to a gridlocked political structure which moves sometimes this way, sometimes that, but without the ability to steer a predictable course clearly and effectively through major issues of our time.

In this book, we will explore this erosion of the ties among ideology, language, and political action. We will describe the role that political language and ambiguity play in developing political direction. We will offer a way to reconnect ideology and action in the context of an analytical system that attempts to locate stability and coherence in political discourse. Based on this analysis, we will gaze into the future to predict the emerging ideology now striving to assume a greater role. We begin by looking at the young twenty-first century and considering the problems of governance and their relationship to political ideology.

MOTIVATING POLITICAL PARTICIPATION

In March 2002, the Center for Political Communication and Civic Leadership at the University of Maryland sponsored a program entitled "Moderation, the Middle, and the Midterms." The panel brought together representatives of both major political parties and activists from nonpartisan issue organizations. As one might expect, all said that a candidate for political office in the United States needed to be somewhat *extreme* to win primaries but then must move to the *center* in the campaign. The interesting thing about a panel whose key terms were "extreme" and "center" was, first, that no one bothered to define the continuum that would give "extreme" and "center" meaning, and second, that the only attempt to identify an ideology that would underlie that continuum was to provide sound-bite issue positions such as "family values" and "gun control." Buzz-word sets such as "family values" and "gun control" are what Kenneth Burke would call a reduction, in fact a synecdoche, the former imprecisely naming values with implied actions elided, the latter imprecisely naming a policy with the values that shape it elided. All rhetoric is, of course, a reduction, but this is a reduction that rings of what Burke has called a Pavlovian reduction. If you ring a bell enough times as you present chickens with their dinner, Burke notes, they will gleefully come running when hearing the bell again, even if this time to their execution.[2]

Now, we suspect any reader can easily identify the political parties that employ each sound bite. The operatives on the panel at the University of Maryland made the case to the students gathered for the program to become involved in political parties because their parties stood for something: one stood for family values and the other for controlling guns. Beyond these buzz words, the panel had little to offer students to help them consider committing themselves to work for the party of their choice. The ability to articulate a political ideology—a perspective transcending the issues of the moment yet enveloping them in a consistent, coherent commitment to values and attitudes—was absent from the discussion.

The program had been organized as a counter to the diminished involvement of students in political activity. Of course, this trend has not only been evident among students. In the 1996, 2000, and 2004 presidential elections, 51.3 percent, 49.1 percent, and 55.1 percent of those eligible participated in the presidential balloting.[3] The percentage has been lower in elections without presidential electors on the ballot. The Republican takeover of the House of Representatives in 1994 was accomplished in an election in which only 38.8 percent of those eligible voted. When asked the reasons for their nonparticipation, some people articulate dissatisfaction with the political system, including disparagement of the honesty and integrity of politicians, disgust with the current state of the political process, and a feeling of impotence in influencing the direction of government through their electoral franchise. Others provide nonpolitical reasons, such as difficulty getting to the polling place or inconvenient hours that do not fit their schedules.[4] All of these explanations reveal a deep lack of engagement in the most minor level of democracy—voting.

Domination by a two-party system suffering diminished citizen involvement further flattens participation. Political parties were originally formed as ideological clusters of citizens and leaders sharing a perspective on fundamental issues of governance. In the early republic, Federalists and Republicans opposed each other in a fundamental dispute about the powers of the federal government and its role in the society. Jefferson's Democratic Republicans were particularly adept at organizing citizens into broad-based rallies with enthusiastic supporters. Jacksonian democracy brought huge crowds to Democratic rallies and celebrating citizens to Washington for the inauguration. By 1840, parades of supporters welcomed candidates for president to venues throughout the country. Throughout American history, third parties, although failing to garner much broad-based electoral support, have formed around strong ideological commitments and involved citizens with enthusiasm for politics.

The identification between most individuals and their political party today generally happens at the time of voter registration. Even then, nearly 40 percent of the electorate identify themselves as independent rather than with a political party, despite the incentive that party identification permits full participation in the primary system.[5] These statistics indicate the weakness of party identification in modern politics. Independence extends to the candidates themselves. Few candidates running for political office below the presidential level regularly associate with a political label in their presentation of their candidacy to voters. The blessing the parties bestow on this practice indicates that the current parties serve more as financing and management mechanisms than they do as sources of identification with voters or with a coherent framework of beliefs, values, and policies.

The result of these trends is the diminished potency of political parties as stages for civic activity. In our time, the parties are indeed big tents, raising big money and setting very general direction. They are homes of convenience to be exploited when beneficial and denied when not. They do not articulate an ideological purpose. They have lost their motivational power for those who seek a role in civic affairs.

UNDISCIPLINED GOVERNMENT AND THE
FAILURE OF THE POLICY APPARATUS

The inability of the political party to translate its functioning into political action can be seen in recent elections. In 1992, Bill Clinton ran for the presidency promising to do something about the system for delivering health care in the United States. Despite his 6 million vote plurality over George H. W. Bush and 202 vote majority in the Electoral College, Clinton's ideological ambiguity and the weak party system failed to translate his victory into similar congressional gains. Nearly 20 million votes went to third-party challenger Ross Perot. Clinton had run for the presidency as a "new Democrat," a label that set him apart from many of his party's candidates who were running for office with their own calculated distance from his ideological positioning. Clinton began governing with a fourteen-vote Democratic Party advantage in the Senate, up one from the balance under his predecessor, and a fifty-two-vote Democratic advantage in the House of Representatives. The advantage in the House was eroded by the loss of nine Democratic seats in the election of 1992. In the phrasing of an earlier electoral era, Clinton's coattails were indeed short. The congressional Democrats were delighted, of course, to have a member of their party in the White House, but their joy was not matched with an ideological commitment that translated into political action.

Following his election, the Clinton administration began developing its health care proposal within the structure of the executive branch. The president appointed Hillary Rodham Clinton to chair a task force charged with developing an acceptable plan. In September 1993, the plan was unveiled in a major campaign of speeches and personal appearances by President Clinton. The development process, however, was a White House operation. The loyalty of Democrats in the Congress would hold as long as public opinion supported the Clinton plan. But the emphasis in the rhetoric of the campaign to sell the plan was on the *problems* presented by the nation's health-care system. Quantification of the uninsured and anecdotes of those burdened with catastrophic illness without insurance to ease the financial burden became the central motivational base for the plan. When it came to the plan itself, there was surprisingly little effort to wrap the specifics of the proposal into an ideological base. Clinton did wave a "Health Care Security Card" during his congressional announcement of the plan to a national audience,[6] invoking memories of Franklin D. Roosevelt's dramatic proposal for Social Security three generations earlier, but he failed to fold his plan into a motivation that would gather support within the Democratic Party or the Democratic caucuses in Congress. Most notably, Clinton offered no defense of his quasi-governmental Health Care Councils.

Soon the Health Insurance Association of America unleashed Harry and Louise, characters in an advertising campaign promoted generally through television. In the ads, an apparently civically involved and informed couple discuss their opinions of the Clinton proposal. The strategy of the ads was simple: admit the difficulties with the health-care system, but target the ideological vacuum by claiming "There must be a better way." Soon Harry and Louise, not the president, defined the bold and innovative Clinton proposal. Public support for the proposal plummeted. When it did, so did the weak Democratic discipline in Congress. On September 23, 1994, Senate Majority Leader George Mitchell declared the Clinton health proposal dead.[7] Six weeks later, the Democratic Party lost nine seats in the Senate and fifty-four seats in the House, thus becoming the minority party in both houses of Congress for the first time in nearly a half-century.

The Republican victory was attributed to Newt Gingrich's "Contract with America." The Contract with America was a mixture of platitudes such as a promise to act "with firmness in the right, as God gives us to see the right," and a list of ten legislative proposals the Republicans promised to enact if they controlled the House.[8] A loosely constructed statement of beliefs and policies, it was hardly a well-rounded statement of conservative principles. However, while launched from a seemingly weak office of House minority leader, Gingrich's contract united many Republicans in the kind of ideological comradeship that made the 1994 election unlike any since at least 1960. But the Republican majorities that emerged from the election were neither large enough nor coherent enough to implement the Contract over Clinton's veto. The new congressional leadership's first legislative victory was an end to Congress's exemption from federal labor laws, hardly a declaration that a new coherent ideology controlled national life. Nor was the discipline present that would continue the unity provided by the weak ideological coherence of the Contract. Two years later, Clinton was reelected with an 8 million vote plurality and a 220 vote majority in the Electoral College. Yet congressional changes in the 1996 election were minimal: the Democrats lost three additional seats in the Senate and gained three seats in the House. Once again the elections turned on individual campaigns by members of Congress and by the president, devoid of strong ideological unity.

In the presidential election of 2000, the Republicans gained control of both houses of Congress and the White House. But the reforms that such a shift would portend have not occurred. Within the Republican margins, despite their more conservative tenor, were a coalition without ideological unity composed of members elected in personal campaigns rather than as part of an ideological choice. The Republican majorities provided little more than solidarity in leadership elections. The majorities evaporated when controversial reforms such as pro-life legislation or budget discipline came before Congress. Indeed, President George W. Bush's greatest triumph on a campaign promise occurred in education, where Democrat Teddy Kennedy became his closest ally in the Senate. Between 1994 when the Republicans gained control of Congress and 2004, the politics of personality engulfed Newt Gingrich and Robert Livingston, who each lost the position of speaker of the House due to hypocrisy on "family values," and Trent Lott was removed as majority leader of the Senate because of his perceived racial insensitivity.

In spite of the unity fostered by September 11 on issues of national security, history points to the inability of the United States government to enact reforms that have been needed for over a generation in health care, the cost of prescription drugs, and the threat of the Baby Boom generation to Social Security and private pension plans. Even issues of the right such as opposition to abortion and to same-sex marriage can muster neither the party discipline nor the ideological motivation to achieve public support. The politics of personality has left congressional parties unable to unify their members and create sufficient public motivational support for their policies. The result has been limited legislation, some with sunset provisions that limit its effective time in place, some pulling the nation right, some left, with political ambiguity the character of the day.

NONIDEOLOGICAL PRESIDENTIAL LEADERSHIP AND THE BETRAYAL OF TRUST

Just as the legislative majority is no guarantee of an ideological commitment to political action, overtly ideological campaigning can create difficulties in responding to changing circumstances. On August 16, 1988, George H. W. Bush accepted the Republican Party nomination for president. In his acceptance speech, he uttered the sort of sound bite that has become the staple of presidential politics: "Read my lips: no new taxes." In the context of the speech, Bush and his speechwriters, notably Peggy Noonan, who had written so well for Ronald Reagan, elaborated the sound bite by contrasting Bush's position with Walter Mondale's more nuanced position on taxes, and including a dramatic and pretended dialogue between Bush and Congress. "The Congress will push me to raise taxes, and I'll say no, and they'll push, and I'll say no, and they'll push again, and I'll say to them, 'Read my lips: no new taxes.' "[9] The tough-sounding pledge created an image of action, specifically aggressive resistance, but was devoid of any attempt to provide an ideological explanation that would provide a context for the pledge. After his election, as Bush's term proceeded, his economic advisers responded to fears of the growing deficits by recommending a tax increase, which Bush signed. Unable to justify his change of policy, because he had provided no ideological justification for his original pledge, Bush was charged with hypocrisy. This was at least one of the factors in the public's judgment that cost him the presidency in 1992: that he could not manage the economy.

Bush's sound bite followed the dominant logic of modern campaigns. During the Republican primaries, Bush often sounded themes that have come to stand in for conservative ideology as he campaigned against a number of opponents, including Jack Kemp, who had made a career as an economic conservative championing tax cuts. Then, while moving to appeals that would attract moderates to his candidacy in the general election so that he could defeat Mondale, Bush still needed to hold the conservatives. The tax pledge was a shortcut to the faithfulness of the economic conservatives in the Republican Party. Other sound bites in the acceptance speech would be lines that other constituencies would recognize. In this pattern of political discourse, little attention is paid to the overall ideology of the various positions. The sound bites do the work of gathering various political orientations to the coalition, but the bonds are narrowly drawn on specific issue promises, not on a deep and wide celebration of shared ideology.

The lesson George H. W. Bush learned is neither unusual nor has it been generally instructive in our politics. In 1992, Bill Clinton told the story of his mother's battle with catastrophic illness. From this personal involvement, he committed to health-care reform that he was not able to deliver. In 2000, George W. Bush ridiculed nation building by the Clinton administration in Somalia and Bosnia-Herzegovina. Then, in Afghanistan and Iraq, the Bush administration became a nation builder with limited results.

One of the fundamental principles of the democratic vote is the bond of trust it establishes between the citizen and the leader. An important building block of such trust is the policy expectations offered during an election campaign. The faith of democracy asserts that, in elections, citizens influence the policies of their government. Yet the linkage between elections and presidential action is not naturally broad. Most of the debate in presidential campaigns, as well as other campaigns for office, revolves around issues that carry neither long memory nor implication into the term. The classic examples of this phenomenon were the issues of Quemoy and Matsu and the missile gap with the Soviet Union that shaped the election of 1960. The former revolved around two islands in the Formosa straits that tested the resolve of the Taiwanese to maintain their independence from mainland China and the American commitment to support that independence. Quemoy and Matsu had been shelled by the Communist Chinese military in 1954 and 1955. They were never shelled again, and American policy did not turn on the stance of protecting them. The latter issue was a charge leveled by John Kennedy against the Eisenhower administration and thus against Richard Nixon, whose campaign was built on his role in that administration. Once Kennedy achieved the presidency, his advisers found no missile gap. In fact, the Soviets were dangerously (from their point of view) behind the United States in missile development and deployment. Their disadvantage at least partially motivated the Soviets to place medium-range missiles in Cuba, which precipitated the Cuban missile crisis. But such issues without legs are present in every campaign.

The major impact of such issues on trust is to place greater focus on promises in the campaign that citizens can clearly see carried into a central role in an administration. Trust is built as actions of an administration are evaluated on the basis of consistency of campaigns with such actions. Thus, issues such as George H. W. Bush's tax pledge and Clinton's health care reform become clear tests of the strength of trust in the administration. By framing these positions narrowly, by choosing to focus their strategies during campaigns on pledges conveyed as sound bites rather than on a broadly based ideology, candidates establish a brittle criterion for the linkage of trust. When they then betray the specifics of their pledges, trust is risked, and the legitimacy and the power of presidencies are endangered.

Furthermore, judgment of a president's performance during his term turns on leadership in the face of events that could not be anticipated at the time of the election. Despite the evidence held in the recesses of the intelligence community and within the White House, how many citizens anticipated the attacks of September 11, 2001? Once those attacks occurred, the nation expected leadership of a kind that was not a part of the political debate in the 2000 campaign. In such unanticipated situations, the legitimacy of presidential action turns again on the trust the citizens have in their leaders.

The inevitable differences between the commitments of a campaign and the reality of governing are one of the motivations for rhetorical framing of an administration's response to situations. George H. W. Bush did not casually betray his promise to veto tax increases. As the economy eroded, he began to realize that the burden of governmental debt was a growing cancer in the economy. The key to continued trust as he reversed his position on the issue was to articulate his justification in such a way that ideology trumped the particular promise—that his conservative supporters would perceive the conservative bases for his actions. But the tax issue had not been presented nor understood in the context of ideology. Nor was the Bush White House capable of justifying the tax increases on the basis of conservative ideology. Bush paid the price of his 1988 strategy even as he performed an action that he believed necessary.

The betrayal of trust weakens presidencies and, with them, presidential leadership. Such betrayals have many roots, but certainly among them are the decisions made by campaigns to embrace campaign discourse that isolates political promise from ideological justification. Such narrowly driven appeals, while they may be successful at the time in defusing opposition or even in attracting support, establish the ticking time bomb of presidential distrust.

THE LOSS OF POLITICAL COALITION

The erosion of trust is not the only difficulty in governing that is created by nonideological discursive strategies. As leaders govern around narrowly defined issues, they govern without a consistent political coalition. Strong political coalitions founded in ideology grant the leader flexibility in policy because they provide a rich background with which the leader can justify policy. Such flexibility is often necessary in the give and take of a legislative process. The freedom to exchange political favors can grease the wheels of legislative accomplishment. Such political favors, however, have the potential to devastate political support, particularly when that political support is based on narrowly defined policy positions.

But sometimes political compromise is less a matter of political favor than it is the way, perhaps the only way, in which a policy can become law. True compromise should let all involved in the compromise reconcile their support for the policy with their ideological interests in the issue. The framing of the issue in the context of ideology provides the flexibility to declare that the principles of the ideology are manifest in the policy. Narrowly drawn policy positions rob the politician of such cover and remove the flexibility from the legislative options.

More perniciously, however, the demands for political compromise carried out and justified within nonideological discourse lead ultimately to the further weakening of the already weak coalitions for governing. They appear as betrayals to those whose membership in the coalition is based on the articulation of oppositions and to those who have expectations defined by their ideological kinship with the leader. Thus, legislative demands create a spiral of disintegration in political coalitions.

The political strategy that creates this ideological chaos is the borrowing or stealing of policy symbols traditionally associated with one's opposition. George W. Bush, for example, has the tendency to increase the role of government, which is inconsistent with the political right's conventional conservative ideology. And Bill Clinton had the tendency to decrease the role of government, which was inconsistent with conventional liberal ideology. Issues on which Bush favors a stronger role for government include abortion, school prayer, and immigration. On the National Mall in Washington, not far from the monument for Thomas Jefferson, George W. Bush embraced the Declaration of Independence, the great document of American liberalism: "The March for Life upholds the self-evident truth of that Declaration—that all are created equal, given the unalienable rights of life, and liberty, and the pursuit of happiness. And that principle of America needs defenders in every place and every generation." Having celebrated American rights, Bush then celebrated his dedication to government policy to constrain women's and scientists' choices: "You and I share a commitment to building a culture of life in America, and we're making progress. As the President, I have signed the Born Alive Infants Protection Act, opposed the destruction of embryos for stem cell research, and refused to spend taxpayer money on international programs that promote abortion overseas."[10]

When the issue is school prayer, Bush also wraps activist government in liberal principles. As governor of Texas, Bush supported organized prayer at football games. The issue is whether the public schools, as agencies of government, can exercise the power of public situations to endorse religious practice. In 2000, the Supreme Court heard a case to decide the legality of student-led prayer at football games after a Texas appeals court struck down a policy allowing Santa Fe High School students to have pregame invocations. Bush wrapped his support for the prayers in the classic liberal rationale of rights. A news report at the time noted, "Bush hopes the court 'will overturn the 5th Circuit's decision because it is a First Amendment right for students to participate in the free exercise of religion,' spokeswoman Linda Edwards told the *Dallas Morning News*."[11]

Bush's position on immigration endorses strong governmental action in support of immigrant communities. Bush has strongly supported federal assistance for the teaching of English as a second language. *A Quality Teacher in Every Classroom* reports "The Language Acquisition portion of No Child Left Behind Act contains a National Professional Development Program that provides discretionary grants to institutions of higher education and schools or States for professional development activities to improve classroom instruction for students learning the English language." The subtlety is that the program is for improving English. Bush supports grants for activities that are "aimed at assisting teachers, administrators, or other educational personnel to meet high professional standards." According to the document, "Last year, President Bush signed legislation that provided $37.5 million for this program in 2002. This year, President Bush has proposed maintaining support for this program in FY-03."[12] The program helps others learn the English language.

English language instruction and immigration are closely related issues. Peter Beinart explains that when Pete Wilson and Pat Buchanan's voices were rising in politics, some observers assumed that the issue of immigration would be used to solidify the political middle, similar to the way affirmative action had been used earlier. According to Beinart, "To some degree, it is big business—with its thirst for immigrant labor—that has kept that from happening. But it is also the historical accident that in 2000 the party chose as its standard-bearer one of its most committed supporters of immigration." Bush questioned Buchanan after a speech in Dallas in 1995, suggesting that Buchanan was picking on friends from the south and opposing bilingual education. According to Beinart, when "Bush tried to restore food stamps to some legal immigrants who lost them in the 1996 welfare bill, most House Republicans opposed him."[13] Regardless of the agreements or disagreements over the positions taken, Bush is borrowing or stealing liberal ideology by advocating policies that increase the role of government in assimilating immigrants.

But perhaps the most obvious of traditionally liberal positions is Bush's expansion of government at the expense of budget deficits. In "Bush Leads Country on Spending Spree," the *Detroit News* reported that Bush increased spending 30 percent in his first three years as president, a sharp contrast with Clinton's 3.5 percent and Reagan's 68 percent in eight years.[14] This indicates that Bush has significantly grown the size of government, which contradicts traditional conservative ideology.

Bush's label for this political positioning is a consciously oxymoronic term: compassionate conservatism. Our point is not that conservatives cannot express or even act from compassion, but that this term floats apart from ideology. The term is designed to reach both ways politically, to the left with a generous, supportive, active government responding to the troubled and unfortunate, and to the right in the identification with conservatism. But the term has no ideological coherence with either right or left. Its thrust is to create ambiguity rather than deep and wide commitment.

Clinton was just as good at borrowing and stealing symbols from other political ideologies, advocating policies that would diminish governmental support for marginalized citizens. The three areas where Clinton contradicted conventional liberal ideology were welfare, an emphasis upon a balanced budget, and family values.

Clinton would steal conservative symbols when dealing with welfare and immigration issues. Beinart explains that it is a fallacy to think that the United States is "immune to the xenophobia that periodically erupts in nations that define themselves in ethnic terms." The conservative sentiment was reluctance to give money to government programs that supported illegal or legal immigration. In 1994, 59 percent of Californians voted to deny health and educational service to illegal immigrants. Two years later, Pat Buchanan won New Hampshire's Republican presidential primary. According to Beinart, "That summer the GOP adopted a positively Buchananesque platform declaring that children born in the United States to foreign parents should no longer automatically become citizens."[15]

Contradicting conventional liberal support for marginalized groups, Clinton enacted legislation that denied food stamps to legal immigrants. According to Beinart, "Clinton did not fight xenophobia on principle; after all, he signed the virulently anti-immigrant welfare bill."[16] The enactment of legislation to reduce government programs of any kind is more a reflection of traditional conservative or reactionary positions than liberal positions. Clinton contradicted conventional liberal ideology to modify that ideology.

Clinton also borrowed or stole from conventional conservative ideology in economic policy. The Clinton administration presided over a tremendous expansion of the economy that generated huge new tax revenues. This largesse promised to fund many programs traditionally championed by liberals. But feeling the heat of economic conservatives charging that he was a "tax and spend liberal," Clinton chose to adopt the conservative call for a tax cut. When Clinton proposed his final budget in 2000, Betsy Dotson noted that his proposal called for "targeted tax cuts costing about $351 billion over 10 years, of which $256 billion are paid for out of the surplus, and the remainder paid for with numerous offsets."[17]

Clinton's economic policy further contradicted liberal ideology with his commitment to a balanced budget. According to Kenneth Walsh and Kent Jenkins Jr., Clinton balanced the budget by relying upon people and the private sector: "Now that Washington has shown some fiscal discipline, President Clinton said, 'The American people and the private sector will grow the economy for us.'"[18] The economy flourished in the Clinton administration, which resulted in a commitment to balance the budget. Walsh and Jenkins explain that balanced budgets have been an expressed goal of politicians since the Eisenhower era, but were usually diverted through faulty plans, idealistic or fantasy economic scenarios, or the inability to reach resolve between the parties. Clinton's emphasis on responsibility for growing the economy stressed the role of the private sector more than the role of government, an emphasis which contradicted conventional liberal ideology.

Clinton also borrowed the symbols of conservative ideology in the area of family values. Ronald Reagan and other conservatives were particularly good at evoking the traditions of family values. Michael J. Sandel explained that Reagan understood the politics of virtue as well as anyone: "He skillfully evoked family and neighborhood, religion and patriotism, even while promoting an unfettered capitalism that undermined the traditions and communities he praised." Other Republicans followed: George H. W. Bush posed in a flag factory and introduced Willie Horton; Dan Quayle criticized Murphy Brown for having a child out of wedlock; William Bennett opposed violent rap music; Pat Buchanan sought to restore country and culture, whatever that means. "Democrats, meanwhile, resisted the politics of virtue, not by disputing conservatives' particular moral judgments but by rejecting the idea that moral judgments have a place in the public realm."[19]

Clinton broke the long-standing pattern that associates family values with conservatives. According to Sandel, Clinton won "as a 'New Democrat' who stressed responsibility as well as rights." He was borrowing the symbols of conservative ideology to win. Nixon won the presidency by standing for law and order, as well as by standing in opposition to a counterculture. Since that time, Sandel suggested, Democrats had not been able to articulate a moral vision. When Clinton came upon the scene, however, he "promoted the V-chip, curfews and school uniforms, and condemned teenage pregnancy, smoking and truancy." Referring to this as "one of the great reversals of contemporary American politics," Sandel explained that Clinton "seized the upper hand in the politics of virtue."[20]

The process we have called the "stealing back and forth of symbols" strikes at the heart of ideological orientation because the embracing of important iconic issues of the opposition weakens the ideological bonds of identification that give political coherence to the opposition. The strategy works in the moment because, like the party recruiters in the auditorium at the University of Maryland, ideology is presented in heavily reduced presentations as issues rather than in a more systematic development of a consistent, coherent commitment to values and attitudes. But, as a symbolic issue is successfully stolen from an alien ideology, it has the ancillary effect of eroding the ideological clarity of the thief. This further intensifies the fragility of the political coalition of the thief. The result is often new efforts to steal symbols and, with them, a few supporters from the opposition. Thus, the cycle deepens. The pattern left behind is an inconsistent tacking from left to right without ideological orientation.

THE FAILURE OF ELECTIONS TO RESOLVE POLITICAL GRIDLOCK

The myth of early twenty-first-century Western democracy is that elections are the magic elixir to cure problems of ambiguity in a culture. Because of momentous elections of the past—Abraham Lincoln's winning of the presidency in 1860, Franklin D. Roosevelt's victory in 1932, and Ronald Reagan's in 1980—election campaigns are viewed as the citizens' choice of direction for governing. In selecting between two political candidates and two political parties championing differing viewpoints on the future, citizens supposedly choose the direction for their government. This is viewed as the time, therefore, when the practitioners of the political art have the opportunity to clarify ideological direction, to present the choice to the electorate, and let the elections establish the direction for government.

But the modern system of election campaigning turns elsewhere for its purpose and leaves campaigns without the power to match this memory of campaigns past. We referred to the political *art* in the paragraph above. Yet the dominant metaphor for politics in our time is not art, but science. The creative molding of political unions and movements through the crafting of campaign discourse is replaced by the careful plotting of polls, focus groups, precision targeting of messages, and pretesting of words and phrases which do not so much mean as stimulate. The science of political campaigning is a domain of experts and technical knowledge bereft of the beauty and inspiration of rhetorical art.

This science is based in three truisms of electoral campaigns. The first is that to assume office the candidate only needs to get more votes than his opponent. Guided by this truism, strategic focus of campaigns narrows to this singular goal. A second truism is that the election campaign is a finite period of time with a fixed end. This truism gives the modern campaign nearsightedness. It is designed to elect, not govern. The third truism is that elections are about candidates. Thus, campaigns designed to promote personality and image subordinate parties, issues, or political direction. Political professionals become experts at packaging that serves to position the candidate rather than to frame policy choice.

The style of the acceptance nights of the two major party conventions of 2004 demonstrate the characteristics of discourse that emerge from this scientific political system. John F. Kerry's acceptance night was a celebration of his Vietnam war service. The candidate was introduced with a film focusing on the events that provided Kerry his credentials as a military hero. The speech began with his biography. We were introduced to his parents, his career, and his wife, even his worthy opponents in the primary campaign. The biography ended with the lessons he had learned in Vietnam that he promised to apply to Iraq. Then Kerry provided a transition to the issues of the campaign[21]:

My fellow citizens, elections are about choices. And choices are about values. In the end, it's not just policies and programs that matter; the president who sits at that desk must be guided by principle. For four years, we've heard a lot of talk about values, but values spoken without actions taken are just slogans. Values are not just words. They're what we live by. They're about the causes we champion and the people we fight for. And it is time for those who talk about family values to start valuing families.

Then follows an arpeggio on the term "values," working from "what we value" to policies that value. "We believe that what matters most is not narrow appeals masquerading as values, but the shared values that show the true face of America. Not narrow appeals that divide us, but shared values that unite us: Family and faith. Hard work and responsibility. Opportunity for all—so that every child, every parent, every worker has an equal shot at living up to their God-given potential." And then the less-than-spellbinder theme of the speech is introduced: "America can do better." Here were a series of words and phrases that had high emotional and affective power—what are called condensation symbols[22]—and which serve no purpose in pointing to a concrete direction for Kerry's policy. These words and phrases transcend the ideology that divides American politics to celebrate values at a level of abstraction void of political philosophy. The candidate is everyman even as he is no one in particular.

When Kerry begins to address specific issues, he presents a mixture of a sympathetic discerning of the problem and a list of isolated characteristics that together compose no coherent plan. A section of the speech concerning health care will suffice to illustrate:

And we value health care that's affordable and accessible for all Americans. Since 2000, four million people have lost their health insurance. Millions more are struggling to afford it. You know what's happening. Your premiums, your co-payments, your deductibles have all gone through the roof.

Our health care plan for a stronger America cracks down on the waste, greed, and abuse in our health care system and will save families up to $1,000 a year on their premiums. You'll get to pick your own doctor—and patients and doctors, not insurance company bureaucrats, will make medical decisions. Under our plan, Medicare will negotiate lower drug prices for seniors. And all Americans will be able to buy less expensive prescription drugs from countries like Canada.

The story of people struggling for health care is the story of so many Americans. But you know what, it's not the story of senators and members of Congress. Because we give ourselves great health care and you get the bill. Well, I'm here to say, your family's health care is just as important as any politician's in Washington, D.C. And when I'm President, America will stop being the only advanced nation in the world that fails to understand that health care is not a privilege for the wealthy, the connected, and the elected—it is a right for all Americans.[23]

Campaign consultant Tony Schwartz has called this style of discourse "the responsive chord."[24] The presentation of the problem is designed to have the listeners see themselves and their neighbors in the problem, but it provides no depth of understanding of the roots of the problem nor narrates its origin. The solution step is a string of careful statements designed to pluck the magic strings that define people's hopes and fears of a solution. In this style of speech, the candidate and his positions emerge crafted into very specific appeals to voters activated by very specific issues. This is not a style that exploits the power of ideology to bond citizens to candidates who commit themselves to leadership of a firm direction for government and inspires listeners to rally to the call to address problems together in a coherent approach.

George W. Bush's acceptance night was a star-drenched spectacle. The theater-in-the-round staging was established to project Bush among the people. His speech opened with a quick tour of scenes of the preceding four years, including the devastation of September 11, 2001, military action, and a thriving economy. Then the speech introduced and praised Bush's wife and parents. Following the appreciation, Bush transitioned into issues: "A presidential election is a contest for the future. Tonight I will tell you where I stand, what I believe, and where I will lead this country in the next four years." This personalization of issues into beliefs structures the next section of the speech. For example, on health care for seniors, Bush said: "I believe we have a moral responsibility to honor America's seniors, so I brought Republicans and Democrats together to strengthen Medicare. Now seniors are getting immediate help buying medicine. Soon every senior will be able to get prescription drug coverage, and nothing will hold us back." Next, Bush entered a section of the speech in which he cataloged actions that would mark his second term. On health care, he offered:

As I've traveled the country, I've met many workers and small-business owners who have told me that they are worried they cannot afford health care. More than half of the uninsured are small-business employees and their families. In a new term, we must allow small firms to join together to purchase insurance at the discounts available to big companies. We will offer a tax credit to encourage small businesses and their employees to set up health savings accounts and provide direct help for low-income Americans to purchase them. These accounts give workers the security of insurance against major illness, the opportunity to save tax-free for routine health expenses, and the freedom of knowing you can take your account with you whenever you change jobs. We will provide low-income Americans with better access to health care. In a new term, I will ensure every poor county in America has a community or rural health center. As I have traveled our country, I've met too many good doctors, especially OB/GYNs, who are being forced out of practice because of the high cost of lawsuits. To make health care more affordable and accessible, we must pass medical liability reform now. And in all we do to improve health care in America, we will make sure that health decisions are made by doctors and patients, not by bureaucrats in Washington, D.C.[25]

The section is strikingly similar in style to Kerry's. The problem is grounded in things he was told as he traveled the country. This is followed by a series of stated policy intentions to fix particular problems and ends with an inoculation strategy about health choice, differing from Kerry's only in that the threatening bureaucrats work for the government rather than for the insurance companies.

The style of these evenings is dictated by the beliefs of the modern campaign organization built from the three truisms we outlined at the beginning of this section: the purpose of a campaign is to collect more votes than the opposition, its responsibilities have a fixed end on election day, and it is about the candidates. Two characteristics dominate these scientific campaigns. First, the campaigns are structured through reduction in language and demographic segmentation of the electorate. Second, the campaigns focus on the image or personality of the candidate.

The campaigns begin with a strategy to identify the groups within the electorate that they will assemble to achieve the plurality of votes on election day. The first cut divides the electorate into three groups: the candidate's base, the opponent's base, and the much smaller portion who might vote for either candidate. In the modern science of elections, this creates a mosaic of strategy that requires (1) activating the candidate's base, (2) attracting the voters that are undecided, and (3) chipping away the base of the opponent. Each of the three broad groups of voters is then analyzed for its possible strategic susceptibilities. With modern communication techniques that segment markets and target messages for specific segments, this complex strategy becomes much easier to accomplish.

A crucial task in a scientifically designed campaign is to hold the base. The dominant belief in the 2004 campaign was that the Republican Party's base is predominantly conservative and the Democratic Party's base is predominantly liberal. But the strategies employed during elections are not designed to build an ideological base, only to hold the base together in the current election. "You are my base," George W. Bush proudly told a large fund-raising gathering. Thus, like the party operatives who seek to motivate students by reciting a mantra of "family values" and "gun control," the campaigns operate with a reduced mantra of symbolic identification of the candidate with issue positions. Issue positions that tie the base to the candidate are identified, and short statements of commitment to those positions are formulated. These are tested in focus groups so they not only resonate with the base, but they also do not drive away the second group, the undecided voter. Just as importantly, wedge issues are developed. Wedge issues are specifically designed to divide the opponent's base from him or her and to keep the candidate's own base from the opposition. In 2004 the issue of same-sex marriage was invoked by Republicans to divide conservative Democrats from the liberal activists who share their party. Similarly, the Democrats exploited the treatment of veterans as an issue that separated a portion of the Republican base from their party. The ideal wedge issue is one that drives up the so-called negatives of the opponent while safely avoiding alienating one's own supporters.

Then the resources of the campaign are allocated to provide messages tested in focus groups to achieve the goals outlined in the analysis. The candidate is scheduled with suitable audiences who will resonate with the message designed for their particular demographics. Media markets are chosen to reach the critical market segments in the states that are in play. Precision planning is the essence of the campaign.

The second characteristic of the modern campaign, its focus on the image or personality of the candidate, comes into play as the campaign chooses discourse that will project certain aspects of the candidate. If George W. Bush is perceived as decisive by the voters his campaign wishes to reach, his campaign should train the candidate to speak decisively. Portray a black and white world where evil must be confronted. Have the candidate promise, "you know where I stand." Have him state his policy plans as what he *will* do in the second term.

These well-developed techniques of modern elections govern the electoral game in the early twenty-first century. The assumptions of these techniques, however, create a political discourse that leads to the ideological vacuum and rudderless political indecision that we have described. The reductive strategies of segmentation and wedge issues work their magic within the confines of an election campaign; they do not create governing coalitions. Appeal to such specific issues without ideological connection leaves the winners governing beyond the election in unanticipated crises without an active legitimacy based in anticipated direction. Thus, the scientific professionalization of campaigns has left politics refined in a direction that separates the symbols of campaigning from the symbols of governing. Each election results in the choice of a candidate, selected as a personality, evaluated by approval ratings, and effective as long as personal ratings remain high. As in the campaign, positions during the leader's term must be measured and chosen with political support in mind. With political support gathered with the scientific techniques of segmentation and reduction, elections no longer serve as benchmark moments when ideological direction points to a new orientation.

THE MEDIA AND CAMPAIGNS

On one typical day in the 2004 presidential campaign, the electronic media featured three stories. First, Speaker of the House Dennis Hastert declared that the country would be in greater danger if John Kerry were elected President. Second, CBS television news was reported to be in deepening trouble because documents with which they supported a story about George W. Bush's National Guard service could not be verified as genuine. Third, John Kerry's campaign management staff was revealed to be changing, with some aides diminished and others coming into influence. The *Washington Post* added a front-page story contrasting the two candidates' positions on Iraq, written to emphasize the changing strategies of the Kerry campaign and the limited success of Bush's campaign in giving comfort that things are going well there. Articles inside the front section reported Democrats' increased pessimism about the campaign and Vice President Dick Cheney's use of fear appeals on the campaign trail. The *Post*'s Outlook section of editorials and opinion carried a story on the differences in the management cultures inside the Democratic and Republican campaigns and a story on the use of issue groups to place ads. None of this coverage could even remotely be portrayed as exploring ideological differences between the candidates or even the ideological bases of either of the campaigns.[26] They reported strategy, personalities, and success or failure.

If the discourses generated by electoral campaigns are characterized by a reduction to winning or losing and a focus on personality, there is little reason to expect that journalists will supply the ideological grounding for those campaigns. In fact, the electronic and print media covering American election campaigns are amazingly consistent in the stories they cover on any given day. They concentrate their coverage on four different story types:

- *The campaign day.* This story reports how the candidates spent their day. At its best, such coverage may include quotations from the speeches given by the candidate that day, or even excerpts in the electronic media. Research shows that the lead and climax of such stories typically are the reporter's judgment on the progress of the campaign.
- *The horse race.* The media coverage is dominated by the story of the campaigns themselves and their successes and failures. The *Post* coverage cited above is dominated by the comings and goings, the strategizing and relative success, even the style of conduct within the campaigns.
- *Issue.* Sometimes campaign coverage explores an issue; sometimes it provides a statement or a comparison of candidate positions. Of the three types of issues—domestic, foreign, and pseudo issues—the latter is by

far the overwhelming coverage. Pseudo issues are those such as John Kerry's Vietnam service or George Bush's National Guard service that have little or no relevance to policy.

- *Personality*. The personality stories give face to campaigns. Typically the coverage identifies and elaborates the life stories of campaign operatives. Candidates may also be profiled this way, but seldom more than once in a campaign.

The latest studies of campaign coverage reaffirm earlier studies that the media's concern is the horse race or strategy coverage; for example, one study of the 2004 campaign found that 72 percent of morning news and 67 percent of evening news coverage was of this type.[27] Doing and reporting campaigns this way does not lend itself to the ideological work that our earlier analysis found missing.

One of the reasons for this dominance is media journalists' conception of their responsibility as revealing the hidden to public scrutiny. The dedication to scoops, being first with the story, remains an essential part of the ethos of journalism. Thus, the intricacies of strategy and planning become the activity in campaigns that fascinates the media. The coverage of one campaign day described above illustrates this motivation.

The dominance of horse-race coverage is also explained by the media's embrace of an identifiable dramatic script for campaign coverage. That script features five different personae:

- *The campaign strategist*. The strategist is portrayed as the thinking, acting, and center of the campaign. The strategist devises plans and messages, deploys resources, and generally manages the campaign. She or he is the center of the drama. The strategists become the celebrities of the campaign coverage. Ronald Reagan's campaigns gave us Michael Deaver. Bill Clinton's gave us James Carville, George Stephanopoulos, and Paul Begala. George W. Bush's gave us Karl Rove. In the campaign drama, the strategists are the protagonists of campaign action.
- *The candidate*. The candidate's job is to carry out the strategies designed by the strategist. Candidates are judged as good or bad candidates by how well they do so. Occasionally the candidates may be given a role in the planning of strategy, but typically they are not portrayed as in charge of their own campaign. For example, a *Washington Post* story reporting on changes in the Kerry campaign organization led with a report on the changes written in the passive so no actor was specified. Not until the fourth paragraph was there a glimmer of Kerry as an actor. That paragraph reported that "Tony Coelho, who was chairman of Al Gore's 2000

presidential campaign, is pushing Kerry" to narrow his list of advisers. The reporter quoted Coelho that "if Kerry tries to be that leader, they're in trouble." The candidate himself announced, "Mary Beth Cahill is running this campaign." An extended account of the failings of the strategists followed.[28]

- *The pollsters.* The pollsters are the scientists of the campaign drama. Their role is to measure the success of the strategies on the responder or voter. Although it is recognized that each campaign has pollster-scientists, the emphasis is on the independent pollsters. The drama requires that they be objective diviners of public opinion.

- *The media.* The media are positioned in this drama as the intermediaries who spread the clever strategist's message to the public. How can we describe the media, who are after all writing these stories, as being manipulated or duped? The strategist succeeds by objectifying "the media." Thus a tension between the volition of the media and its subordination to the strategist opens in the accounts. The media must surrender control to make the drama work, and reporters writing from this perspective do so. In this drama, media members who become too active are charged with bias because they step out of their role as conduits of the strategist's message.

- *The reactant.* In the drama, the role of the reactant is to verify the success or failure of the campaign strategy. During the progress of the campaign, the reactant is presented as the responder to opinion polls. Of course, the ultimate test of strategy occurs on election day when voters are portrayed as respondents to the strategy. After the election, the drama performs a detailed analysis of the strategies of the campaign, portraying the reactants in the detailed analysis of voting patterns. Throughout the drama, reactants may be described demographically. Recently, print media have even featured reports of focus groups of possible voters. In media stories, the electorate is seldom portrayed as making decisions about policy or direction of government before or after the election. Rather, the media's interest in the electorate is tied to the voters' response to the candidates and their strategies.

In the plot of the drama, the strategists assess the reactants and plan a strategy designed to move them to support their candidate. The candidate delivers the message with or without skill, effectively or ineffectively. The media disseminate the strategist's messages with or without distortion, resisting or implementing the strategy. The pollsters assess the effect on reactants. From the assessments of these polls, the strategist's plan evolves.

This drama becomes the framework within the media for assigning stories and reporting campaigns. Questions of ideology disappear, except when they occasionally appear in conjunction with strategic design or media bias. The coverage is dominated by who's up, who's down, who's in, who's out. This drama reduces elections in several ways. First, the election becomes confined by the truism that its termination is election day. Thus, elections are seldom seen as citizens' opportunity to select the direction for their government. Certainly, long-term concepts such as ideology are beyond the scope of the coverage. Second, the drama reduces citizens to the role of absorbers and responders to messages of the campaign. Thus, no active role for citizens as choosers of direction for government is portrayed during the course of the campaign. Such stories may be told after the campaign, but they do not structure campaign coverage. Voters viewing media coverage of modern campaigns will *not* see their exercise of the vote motivated by their role in selecting the direction for government. Third, the drama reduces the candidates to implementers of short-term strategy, thus denying them a role as the carriers of ideology from public into government. The result is the diminishment of ideology in the election process that we have highlighted. The style diminishes the potential of elections to halt ambiguous drift. Its fruits are the lack of civic motivation, of political power, and the eroded trust in governing that we have described.

THE SHIFTING SEARCH FOR IDEOLOGIES OF SECURITY

The horrendous events of September 11, 2001, magnified the ideological chaos that already dominated American politics and presented unanticipated demands on the motivations for political leadership. On that day, the calm sense of order in the United States was destroyed when terrorists hijacked four airliners and flew three of them into symbols of American power. Unlike during other hijackings, these terrorists did not intend to take hostages and negotiate for political or monetary demands: they were on a suicide mission. Who could forget the images? Two planes crashed into the World Trade Center, one into the Pentagon, and the last into a Pennsylvania field. The devastating impact of the terrorism echoed for days as normal life came to a halt. People were glued to media outlets that repeated slow-motion images of the collapsing Twin Towers.

The events of 9/11 were sensational and in every sense the rhetorical situation described by Lloyd Bitzer, demanding rhetorical response.[29] Public chaos and outrage demanded that political and cultural leaders step forward, speak, inform, give meaning to the events, channel the outrage, and restore stability to the nation. To receive domestic support for actions to come, leaders in all such times must call upon the nation's ideology to justify their choice of response to the situation. Different ideologies draw upon different geometries of power to frame events such as this. One ideology attributes such an act to individuals, labels it a crime, and invokes the criminal justice system as a framework for response. This structure reaffirms the security of the social order by isolating those who are culpable, surrounding them with the investigative power of the state to fix responsibility, presenting the case to a court, and obtaining the conviction that assures justice for the victims. Upon first hearing of the events of the morning of September 11 while visiting an elementary school in Florida, George W. Bush invoked the criminal framework, committing the government "to conduct a full-scale investigation to hunt down and to find those folks who committed this act."[30]

But soon, Bush muted the ideology that invoked the criminal justice system in favor of the second ideology: military action in defense of the nation. American ideology and international law provide rationale for the United States when attacked by a foreign enemy to defend itself with military action. The military motivational structure restores security not through the isolation and punishment of offenders provided by the criminal justice motive, but rather through the exercise of the culture's power against a formidable enemy who can only be overcome by extraordinary concentrations of power in government. The military is a very different institution than the courts, structured in ways that authorize different actions. Because the relative power of government and enemy is more comparable than government and criminal, the government uses the military motive to gather greater power around it. Citizens are called out of domestic life into service. Democratic rights are abridged as threatening the war effort. Dissent is silenced as comfort to the enemy. The growth of government power is justified within the defensive war ideology by the fear of danger to the nation and the need for concentration of power to match the power of the enemy and restore security.

In a short statement to the nation from Barksdale Air Force Base in Louisiana, where Air Force One flew after leaving Florida, Bush began to shift the motivation for response from crime to war. Although he began by promising "The United States will hunt down and punish those responsible for these cowardly acts," he also assured that "Our military at home and around the world is on high alert status."[31] By September 20, 2001, after climbing through the layers of real and symbolic rubble, Bush decided to address a joint meeting of Congress and call upon the ideology of defense to put the nation at war. In that speech, he described the horror of September 11 and specified what should be done in response. "On September 11, enemies of freedom committed an act of war against our country. Americans have known wars, but for the past 136 years they have been wars on foreign soil, except for one Sunday in 1941. Americans have known the casualties of war, but not the center of a great city on a peaceful morning." In these opening statements, Bush characterized the horror and significance of the act and framed it as an act of war directed toward the American people. This was an early sign that his ideological framing would be intrinsically tied to the language used to justify a "war on terrorism."

Bush continued by offering the nation direction: "We will direct every resource at our command—every means of diplomacy, every tool of intelligence, every instrument of law enforcement, every financial influence and every necessary weapon of war." Bush said: "Our nation, this generation, will lift the dark threat of violence from our people and our future. We will rally the world to this cause by our efforts, by our courage. We will not tire, we will not falter, and we will not fail."[32] Bush's language personified the unified determination of the country. Then he added the phrase "every necessary weapon of war." In declaring war against the "terrorists," Bush chose the ideology of warfare over the ideology of criminal justice—investigation, prosecution, and conviction. Bush declared an enemy, vilified him, magnified the challenge he presented, and targeted him for the full efforts of American military might.

This initial shift from the ideology of crime to the ideology of defensive war was successful. Bush satisfied the rhetorical demands of the defensive war ideology. Public support measured by the *Washington Post*/ABC News poll showed 90 percent approval for Bush's commitment to respond against Afghanistan.[33] There were few doubts that the extremist organization al Qaeda and its leader Osama bin Laden were the attackers. The war in Afghanistan began, and the Taliban government that had supported al Qaeda was overthrown. Given this framework in the ideology of defensive war, the world accepted American actions as appropriate, just, and legitimate. French President Jacques Chirac expressed outrage at the terrorists' actions on 9/11 and assured the United States of France's support and sympathy. "France is deeply upset to learn of the monstrous attacks that have just struck the United States. In these terrible circumstances, all French people stand by the American people. We express our friendship and solidarity in this tragedy." German Chancellor Gerhard Schroeder said: "the German people stand by the United States of America at this difficult hour." At a special meeting, European Union foreign ministers issued a statement: "There will be no safe haven for terrorists and their sponsors, the Union will work closely with the United States and all partners to combat international terrorism."[34] This support continued through the military action in Afghanistan. The United Nations Security Council passed a resolution supporting the establishment of the International Security Assistance Force (ISAF). According to the ISAF, approximately 5,500 ISAF troops from 33 countries were stationed in Afghanistan as of January 2004.[35]

But by the State of the Union Address on January 29, 2002, Bush's ideological commitment to defensive war was being expanded beyond a defensive war against al Qaeda to other parts of the world.[36] Adding to the list of potential enemies, Bush named Iran, Iraq, and North Korea as an "Axis of Evil." It was generally assumed that Iran was a state sponsoring terrorism; Iraq was building and concealing nuclear, chemical, and biological weapons; and North Korea was creating the infrastructure for building missiles and other suspect technology. Evil was given new faces, so the military quest could continue. But the links between the new faces and terror were not direct. The ideology that supported defensive war, domestically and internationally, was not satisfied. None of these nations had attacked the United States. They may have threatened, thus justifying targeting by American diplomacy, but the "just war" doctrine that constituted the legitimate justification for defensive war did not lift them to legitimate targets of war, declared or undeclared.

As the Bush administration began to frame its argument for war with Iraq, the search for a valid ideology to properly motivate the war began. In the foreign policy debate on October 11, 2000, Bush had campaigned against what he called "nation building." In the same debate, Bush elaborated, "I'm not so sure the role of the United States is to go around the world and say, 'This is the way it gotta be.' We can help. And maybe it's just our difference in government—the way we view government. I mean, I want to empower people. I don't—you know, I want to help people help themselves, not have government tell people what to do. I just don't think it's the role of the United States to walk into a country, say, 'We do it this way; so should you.' "[37] Together these statements established an expectation of reluctance to shed American blood and treasure in replacing governments around the world. But from the beginning, the Bush administration's foreign policy apparatus was developing such plans for Iraq. In January 2004, former treasury secretary Paul O'Neill described plans for the Iraq war that predated 9/11.[38] In 2002, the effort began to hitchhike on 9/11 in the service of overthrowing the Saddam Hussein regime in Iraq. As war with Iraq drew close, the Bush administration began a chaotic search for legitimacy for its effort to replace Hussein and build a democratic Iraq in the reversal of its campaign commitment.

The first strategy was to expand the successful defensive war ideology to cover Iraq. In September 2002, the Bush administration issued *The National Security Strategy of the United States* as the primary statement of policy on use of force by the United States government.[39] That document asserted an expanded doctrine for a just war. It first of all stressed the historical exceptions to the self-defense criterion of the just war doctrine, then used that precedent along with the increased devastation wrought by weapons of mass destruction to justify a policy of legitimate preemption of threat. Preemption of threat was an abandonment of the dominant international ideology of defensive war: war was justified only in response to attack. Using this doctrine, Bush began to justify war with Iraq based on Iraq's reported possession of weapons of mass destruction. The Bush administration approached the United Nations and requested a resolution concerning the Iraqi weapons. The United Nations responded by reestablishing a weapons inspection system.

On September 12, 2002, a year and a day after 9/11, Bush addressed the United Nations. There he introduced a new justification for war against Iraq: "The conduct of the Iraqi regime is a threat to the authority of the United Nations, and a threat to peace. Iraq has answered a decade of UN demands with a decade of defiance. The entire world now faces a test, and the United Nations a difficult and defining moment. Are Security Council resolutions to be honored and enforced, or cast aside without consequence? Will the United Nations serve the purpose of its founding, or will it be irrelevant?"[40] The statement and the speech tapped a second ideology—the necessity of credibility of threat for government to be meaningful—to set the United States up as the enforcer of United Nations credibility. The UN Security Council, of course, asserted its primary stewardship for the credibility of the United Nations and insisted that the inspection system play out to the end.

By the State of the Union Address on January 28, 2003, Bush had returned to his expanded doctrine of preemptive war and to the Iraqi weapons program. There he made the case for the threat of Iraqi weapons of mass destruction based on the testimony of Iraqi dissidents seeking American support to overthrow Saddam Hussein, the dubious British reports of the purchase of uranium from Africa, and intelligence reports that turned out to be flawed.[41] Shortly thereafter, on February 5, 2003, Colin Powell presented the case against Iraq to the UN Security Council. He presented elaborate graphics of what Iraqi weapons systems were thought to look like, interpreted conversations of Iraqi governmental officials, and presented a case that failed to persuade the United Nations to act.[42]

Stephen Toulmin's analytic system[43] for evaluating argument highlights the elements of Bush's search for legitimacy in the speeches. The evidence Bush outlined, and that presented by Colin Powell at the UN, constituted the data to support the claim. The warrant for the argument relied on the expanded defensive war argument for preemptive war. In the end, the world decided that neither the data nor the warrant was compelling. American public opinion, bathed in the insecurity following 9/11, at first supported the Iraq war. Support eroded as data were proven false and the arguments of those who opposed preemptive war became more potent.[44]

For many, the turn of attention to Iraq represented an abandonment of the centrality of the war on terrorism. This is debatable. But what is clearly the case is that the United States had changed the ideological basis for its world actions. In attempting to expand the just war doctrine and in threatening the Security Council that the United States would enforce UN resolutions even if the Security Council did not endorse its actions, the United States abandoned the accepted ideology of the just defensive war.

With that action, American support around the world began to diminish. Threats of vetoes by three of the five permanent members of the Security Council, including NATO allies France and Germany, precluded UN support for the war. In "America and Anti-Americans," Salman Rushdie observed: "In spite of the military successes, America finds itself facing a broader ideological adversary that may turn out to be as hard to defeat as militant Islam: anti-Americanism, which is presently becoming more evident everywhere." Rushdie stated that the Bush administration had come a long way, but it should not abandon consensus building and ignore the rest of the world.[45] America needed to exercise its power responsibly. An article in the *Japan Times* by Eric Teo Chu Cheow indicated that an anti-American sentiment was growing in China because of the Bush administration's unilateralism and emphasis on a war on terrorism. In the same article, Teo Chu Cheow reported: "A recent poll of 38,000 people in 44 countries, conducted by the nonpartisan Pew Research Center in association with the *International Herald Tribune*" found "not only a strong public opposition in Muslim countries toward an eventual war on Iraq, but also a rising anti-American tide."[46] Bush's Lone Ranger attitude also infuriated people at home. In January 2003, nearly 1 million people gathered in Washington, D.C., to protest a potential war with Iraq.

On March 19, 2003, the United States invaded Iraq. The overwhelming power of the American military, a well-developed battle plan, and a weakened enemy army led to a quick overthrow of Hussein's regime. But international support for the war did not follow. UN Secretary General Kofi Annan told the BBC that "the US-led invasion of Iraq was an illegal act that contravened the UN Charter."[47] Once the U.S. Army and Marines had taken control of Iraq, no stockpiles of weapons of mass destruction were found. In 2004 the 9/11 Commission reported that there was no evidence linking Iraq with 9/11.[48] Bush's efforts at nation building proved no more effective than Clinton's. In June 2004, public opinion polls found that a slim plurality of those questioned in the United States did not consider the Iraq war a mistake.[49]

In the face of this crisis of credibility, the Bush administration turned to a third ideology to justify the war: the American mission to democratize the world. The ideology was as old as the American Puritans' "errand into the wilderness," secularized during the American Revolution, to see the United States as a nation founded to serve as the bulwark of democracy to the world. The military plan for Iraq was entitled "Operation Iraqi Freedom." The administration's predictions that American troops would be met by Iraqis cheering their liberation stemmed from the ideology. With the other justifications for the war crumbling around him, Bush began to justify the Iraq war as providing the blessings of freedom to the Iraqi people. In a press conference on April 13, 2004, Bush explained, "I also have this belief, strong belief, that freedom is not this country's gift to the world; freedom is the Almighty's gift to every man and woman in this world. And as the greatest power on the face of the Earth, we have an obligation to help the spread of freedom."[50] Like the Puritans, Bush called upon the obligation to do God's work to motivate support for the war.

We have earlier warned of the dangers of nonideological discourse, which is better rephrased as discourse without compass, or as ideology without reflection, understanding, and accountability. The ideology that people and nations implement has consequences for the present and for projections into the future. The war on Iraq is a lesson. The carefully orchestrated justification for military action in Afghanistan that followed 9/11 succeeded because it showed an awareness of the ideological roots of the just war doctrine and its support for defensive warfare. When the administration turned to Iraq, their justification required a turn from that accepted ideology. But the administration again found itself wanting for a consistent ideological justification for the war. They tried to expand the defensive war justification. They portrayed the war as a service to a United Nations that condemned it. They abandoned the campaign pledge to avoid nation building in favor of a pledge to bring the blessings of freedom and liberty to Iraq and the greater Muslim world. With such inconsistency of position, the administration's effort failed, leaving the United States immersed in a chaotic Iraq without international support. The price of ideological ignorance was once again paid, this time with American treasure and blood.

SITUATING IDEOLOGY IN POLITICAL DISCOURSE

We have examined a number of the costs of the diminished presence of ideological context in American political discourse. C. K. Ogden and I. A. Richards, particularly in their conceptualization of the word-thought-thing triangle of meaning, have taught us that all discourse reduces its subject matter.[51] Meaning is created in relation to the words, the thoughts or psychological context, and the things or referents. The word *dog* is not the thing dog, and each person has experiences with an actual dog that are different from others. Kenneth Burke explains that "any terminology of motives reduces the vast complexity of life by reduction to principles, laws, sequences, classifications, correlations, in brief, abstractions or generalizations of one sort or another."[52] But a style of rhetorical invention that views words as simple stimulus-response, or as Tony Schwartz describes, striking the responsive chords, is dramatically different from a style that views words as the materials from which shared understanding of events are constructed and actions guided, or as Burke describes, "rounded statements about motives."[53] The former is based on a simple relationship of correspondence between words and things and an affective response. The latter requires a complex set of connections and relationships that connect particular moments to memory, description, evaluation, and action. Effective long-term political discourse judged not in terms of its usefulness to a politician in the present moment but in its service to the long-term viability of democracy must, in each moment, present the world as a plausible place, respond to that plausible world in ways that will accept it or change it, and do so in ways that bring citizens into support of and participation in the public responses. Ideology provides the structures of understanding that unite disparate citizens in effective political action.

While useful to and often effective for advertisers, political leaders, and social protestors, reductions can be problematic when given such a grand burden as we have described. Burke explains that such terms as Elizabethanism or capitalism indeed "sum up a vast complexity of conditions which might conceivably be reduced to a near-infinity of positive details; however, if you succeeded in such a description you would find that your recipe contained many ingredients not peculiar to 'Elizabethanism' or 'capitalism' at all."[54] Similarly, reductions such as "Just Do It" and "Be All That You Can Be" have very different meanings and implications for the people who use them. Emotionally laden terms, phrases, and slogans are useful as abbreviations and summations at the level of generalization, but they are inherently imprecise and problematic at the level of particularization, creating ideological confusion.

Many presidents have used reductions in mustering support for the policy initiatives of their administrations. Theodore Roosevelt's "Square Deal," Franklin D. Roosevelt's "New Deal," and Harry S. Truman's "Fair Deal" are examples. "Deals" are pacts, arrangements, and agreements between the parties bonded in the act. The Square Deal was about the earlier idea of labor, citizenship, parenthood, and Christian ethics, while the New Deal was about taking action to bring about immediate economic relief and reform for industry, agriculture, finance, and labor.

Later presidents became fond of simpler slogans to frame their action, and the media multiplied this tendency. John F. Kennedy was on the edge of a "New Frontier." He had to overcome religious bias to become the first Catholic elected president, and he had to fend off communism during the Cuban missile crisis. Lyndon B. Johnson proclaimed his vision of a "Great Society" and declared a "war on poverty" while deflecting voices of protest during the Vietnam War. Richard M. Nixon became the first president to resign from office because of the "Watergate Scandal," and Gerald R. Ford supported the idea of "Unity" before Jimmy Carter promised an "America as good as its People." The "Great Communicator" Ronald Reagan described America as that "Shining City on a Hill." George H. W. Bush asked people to "read my lips: no new taxes," and Bill Clinton became infamously associated with the phrase "Bridge to the Twenty-first Century." While Al Gore wanted to be "Working for America," the eventual worker for America was George W. Bush, who had initially campaigned as a "Compassionate Conservative." Some of these slogans do legitimate reductive work, capturing an ideology and uniting the public in support of the actions of a president and his government. Others win an election but are soon destroyed on the rocks of hard politics.

Our goal is to provide a method or a technique for attaining depth and breadth in political communication. We seek to consider ways of inventing and understanding messages that have the ideological richness to do the hard work that politics demands. Our call is not for longer messages, although longer forms might become more prominent. Nor is our call for more rational messages, although our approach stresses relationship or ratios in discursive practices, and thus implies a greater prominence of reasoning and reason giving. Our call is instead for a rethinking of the rhetorical theory driving political discourse. We urge a greater concern in political discourse for considering public problems in terms of the democratic goals. To do this, we need to understand the power of words beyond their referential accuracy or their affective strength. We have to view the complexity of political discourse and the connections fostered by effective grounding in powerful cultural ideology.

CONCLUSION

We have argued that political positions in the United States today are ideologically chaotic and that there are significant prices to pay for that chaos. We have identified problems in the viability of democratic government tied to the inability of political leaders and institutions to respond powerfully to events around them. We have examined the characteristics of current political discourse that preclude the breaking of the gridlock that this chaos has caused. We have also examined the critical issue of war and peace in which the Bush administration has developed justifications grounded in ideology, but with a confusion born of ineffective strategy and misunderstanding of the demands of the ideologies they invoke.

Nations can tolerate a rudderless political system for a time. At some point, however, problems begin to demand solution. Gridlock must give way to direction. Timely engagement on the issues of the day can prevent periods of national trial and disunity. The United States has not reached a crisis yet in the gridlock at the beginning of the twenty-first century. But predicting when the current generation will face the kinds of difficulties faced in earlier times of crisis such as the Civil War, the Great Depression, or World War II is a difficult task. When that time comes, leaders with a facility in communicating to foster understanding, political unity, and skilled direction in responding to the crisis will be a vital concern. We seek to assist in that revitalization of political discourse.

In the chapters that follow, we examine the nature of political ideology and democratic government more closely. We provide a framework for understanding the relationship of discourse to ideology, and we illustrate this framework with examples. Finally, we examine the future of a sound political discourse.

NOTES

1. An exception substitutes geography for color to designate the political divide. See John Sperling, *The Great Divide: Retro versus Metro America* (Sausalito, Calif.: PoliPoint Press, 2004).

2. Kenneth Burke, *Permanence and Change: An Anatomy of Purpose*, 3rd ed. (1935; Berkeley: University of California Press, 1984), 6.

3. Although there is dispute about the figure for 2004, data indicate around 60 percent voted in that election.

4. United States Census Bureau, *Voting and Registration in the Election of November 1996* (July 1998), www.census.gov/prod/3/98pubs/p20-504/pdf (September 26, 2004).

5. *National Election Studies* (1995–2000), Center for Political Studies, University of Michigan, Ann Arbor, www.umich.edu/~nes (December 15, 2004). The University of Michigan's National Election Survey has tracked party identification since 1952. When given the opportunity to respond on a seven-point scale (strong Democrat, weak Democrat, Independent leaning Democratic, Independent without preference, Independent leaning Republican, weak Republican, strong Republican), 36 percent of respondents in 2002 identified themselves as independent, 34 percent as either strong or weak Democrats, and 30 percent as either strong or weak Republicans. In 1952, 23 percent identified as independent, 47 percent Democratic, and 28 percent Republican.

6. The White House, Office of the Press Secretary, "Address of the President to the Joint Session of Congress" (September 22, 1993), www.ibiblio.org/nhs/supporting/remarks-final.html (January 7, 2005).

7. A detailed account of the fate of the Clinton health care plan is reported in Haynes Johnson and David S. Broder, *The System: The American Way of Politics at the Breaking Point* (Boston: Little, Brown, 1996).

8. National Center for Public Policy Research, www.nationalcenter.org/Contract withAmerica.html (September 24, 2004).

9. George H. W. Bush, "1988 Republican National Convention Acceptance Address" (August 18, 1988), Republican National Convention, New Orleans, La., www.americanrhetoric.com/speeches/georgehbush1988rnc.htm (September 24, 2004).

10. The White House, "President Speaks at 30th Annual March for Life on the Mall" (January 22, 2003), www.whitehouse.gov/news/releases/2003/01/20030122-3.html (January 27, 2003).

11. "Student Prayer Case Reaches Supreme Court," *Techniques*, February 2000, 8.

12. The White House, "A Quality Teacher in Every Classroom: Improving Teacher Quality and Enhancing the Profession" (January 28, 2003), www.whitehouse.gov/infocus/education/teachers/quality_teachers.html (December 5, 2004).

13. Peter Beinart, "TRB from Washington: Quiet Time," *New Republic*, May 13, 2002, 6.

14. "Bush Leads Country on Spending Spree," *Detroit News*, December 28, 2003, A17.

15. Beinart, "TRB from Washington," 6.

16. Beinart, "TRB from Washington," 6.

17. Betsy Dotson, "President Clinton Submits FY 2001 Budget," *Government Finance Review* 16 (April 2000): 2, 55.

18. Kenneth T. Walsh and Kent Jenkins Jr., "The Deal of a Generation: A Five-year Plan to Get to a Balanced Budget," *U. S. News and World Report*, May 12, 1997, 50.

19. Michael J. Sandel, "Easy Virtue," *New Republic*, September 2, 1996, 23.

20. Sandel, "Easy Virtue," 23.

21. John Kerry, "Speech to the 2004 Democratic National Convention" (July 29, 2004), www.johnkerry.com/pressroom/speeches/spc_2004_0729.html (September 24, 2004).

22. W. Lance Bennett, "The Ritualistic and Pragmatic Bases of Political Campaign Discourse," *Quarterly Journal of Speech* 63 (1977): 219–38.

23. Kerry, *Speech*.

24. Tony Schwartz, *The Responsive Chord* (Garden City, N.Y.: Anchor Books, 1972).

25. George W. Bush, "2004 Republican National Convention Address" (September 2, 2004), www.americanrhetoric.com/speeches/convention2004/georgewbushrnc.htm (September 24, 2004).

26. Coverage for Sunday, September 19, 2004, is described.

27. "Network News Coverage of '04 Primaries Falls Short, Study Finds," *Alliance for Better Campaigns: Political Standard*, May 2004, www.ourairwaves.org/standard/display.php?StoryID=314 (November 24, 2004). The study also found that the exception to this coverage pattern is the Sunday morning news programs, where issue coverage does dominate. The study did not report the type of issue covered. Past studies finding the same characteristics in politics over the last thirty years include: James F. Klumpp, Daniel Sullivan, and Dennis Garrett, "The Issue-Image Dichotomy: A Study of Political Communication and TV News" (presented at the Central States Speech Association Convention, Detroit, Mich., April 1977); Thomas E. Patterson and Robert D. McClure, *The Unseeing Eye: The Myth of Television Power in National*

Elections (New York: Putnam, 1976); William C. Adams, ed., *Television Coverage of the 1980 Presidential Campaign* (Norwood, N.J.: Ablex, 1983); Michael J. Robinson and Margaret A. Sheehan, *Over the Wire and on TV: CBS and UPI in Campaign '80* (New York: Russell Sage Foundation, 1983); Joseph N. Capella and Kathleen Hall Jamieson, *Spiral of Cynicism: The Press and the Public Good* (New York: Oxford, 1997); Thomas E. Patterson, *The Vanishing Voter: Public Involvement in an Age of Uncertainty* (New York: Knopf, 2002); Kathleen Hall Jamieson and Paul Waldman, *The Press Effect: Politicians, Journalists and the Stories That Shape the Political World* (New York: Oxford, 2003).

28. Mark Leibovich and Jim VandeHei, "New Blood at Heart of Kerry Campaign; Some See Changes as a Last Chance," *Washington Post*, September 17, 2004, A1.

29. Lloyd F. Bitzer, "The Rhetorical Situation," *Philosophy and Rhetoric* 1 (1968): 1–14.

30. George W. Bush, "Today We've Had a National Tragedy," Remarks at Emma Booker Elementary School, Sarasota, Fla. (September 11, 2001), www.american-rhetoric.com/speeches/gwbush911florida.htm (November 28, 2004).

31. George W. Bush, "Freedom Itself Was Attacked This Morning," Remarks at Barksdale Air Force Base, La. (September 11, 2001), www.americanrhetoric.com/speeches/gwbush911barksdale.htm (November 28, 2004).

32. The White House, "President Bush Addresses Congress and the Nation" (September 20, 2001), www.whitehouse.gov/news/releases/2001/09/20010920-8.html (June 15, 2004).

33. Richard Morin and Claudia Deane, "Bush Has Wide Support in Crisis, Poll Shows," *Washington Post*, September 23, 2001, A16.

34. Collected with the statements of other world leaders, www.september11news.com/InternationalReaction.htm (September 24, 2004).

35. "Afghanistan: Still No Peace," Canadian Broadcasting Corporation (September 24, 2004), www.cbc.ca/news/features/afghanistan_sagacontinues.html (December 15, 2004).

36. The White House, "President Bush Addresses Congress and the Nation" (January 29, 2002), www.whitehouse.gov (June 15, 2004).

37. George W. Bush, "The Second Gore-Bush Presidential Debate" (October 11, 2000), www.debates.org/pages/trans2000b.html (September 24, 2004).

38. Ron Suskind, *The Price of Loyalty: George W. Bush, the White House, and the Education of Paul O'Neill* (New York: Simon and Schuster, 2004).

39. *National Security Strategy of the United States* (Washington: GPO, 2002), www.whitehouse.gov/nsc/nss.html (September 24, 2004).

40. The White House, "President's Remarks to the United Nations General Assembly" (September 12, 2002), www.whitehouse.gov/news/releases/2002/09/20020912-1.html (September 24, 2004).

41. The White House, "President Delivers 'State of the Union' " (January 28, 2002), www.whitehouse.gov/news/releases/2003/01/20030128-19.html (January 7, 2005).

42. The White House, "U.S. Secretary of State Colin Powell Addresses the U.N. Security Council" (February 5, 2003), www.whitehouse.gov/news/releases/2003/02/20030205-1.html (September 24, 2004).

43. Stephen Toulmin, *The Uses of Argument* (Cambridge: Cambridge University Press, 1958).

44. Public Opinion by the Harris Poll showed Bush's support on Iraq peaking in April 2003 at 67 percent. By June 2004, only 41 percent of the public expressed approval of Bush's handling of the war. David K. Krane, *Harris Poll*, No. 47, Table 1 (June 30, 2004), www.harrisinteractive.com/harris_poll/index.asp?PID=476 (January 8, 2005).

45. Salmon Rushdie, "America and Anti-Americans," *New York Times*, February 4, 2002, final edition, A23.

46. Eric Teo Chu Cheow, "Anti-Americanism Rises in Asia," *Japan Times*, 11 January 2003, Lexis-Nexis (April 7, 2003).

47. "Iraq War Illegal, Says Annan," British Broadcasting Service (September 16, 2004), http://news.bbc.co.uk/2/hi/middle_east/3661134.stm (September 24, 2004).

48. Walter Pincus and Dana Milbank, "Al Qaeda–Hussein Link Is Dismissed," *Washington Post*, June 17, 2004, A1. See also Dana Priest, "Al Qaeda–Iraq Link Recanted: Captured Libyan Reverses Previous Statement to CIA Officials Say," *Washington Post*, August 1, 2004, A20.

49. Krane, *Harris Poll*, No. 47, Table 3 (June 30, 2004), www.harrisinteractive.com/harris_poll/index.asp?PID=476 (January 8, 2005).

50. The White House, "President Bush Addresses the Nation in Prime Time Press Conference" (April 13, 2004), www.whitehouse.gov/news/releases/2004/04/20040413-20.html (September 24, 2004).

51. C. K. Ogden and I. A. Richards, *The Meaning of Meaning*, 8th ed. (New York: Harcourt, Brace, 1946), 11.

52. Kenneth Burke, *A Grammar of Motives* (1945; Berkeley: University of California Press, 1969), 96.

53. Burke, *A Grammar of Motives*, xv.

54. Kenneth Burke, *A Rhetoric of Motives* (1950; Berkeley: University of California Press, 1969), 184.

2

Political Ideology and Democracy

In chapter 1, we described the problems that have followed the growth of political communication practices that separate messages from the political ideology in which they are grounded. Our indictment left unanswered some vital questions: Why is ideology important to a democracy? If the use of political terms such as conservative and liberal seem so destructive in our modern politics, why do we need to worry about ideology at all? Why not leave the concept behind and search for a nonideological alternative?

This chapter answers those questions by examining the importance of ideology in democracy. We will argue that the notion of political ideology inheres in democracy in general and American democracy in particular. The United States has a rich history of creating a shared political culture supported by the strong identification of its citizens with one another and a shared sense of national purpose. This culture has generally been achieved through the conjoining of interests and individuals who have persuaded one another to accept a shared perspective on the functioning of public life. In this process of collaboration, collectivity, and consensus, ideology performs vital functions. Its erosion in our time is one of the reasons American democracy is in such a precarious condition. In practice, the terms we will encounter within this discussion—including *ideology*, *political philosophy*, and even *democracy*—are often employed more as rallying cries than as a precise language. Properly grounded in ideology, however, they are what Michael Calvin McGee has called "ideographs": words or phrases, employed in real discourse, having meaning not through precise material reference but because of the ideological work that they do, functioning clearly and evidently to develop, articulate, or celebrate political consciousness.[1] Thus, we do not want to define them precisely either, but we do want to provide a rationale for the contribution of ideology to political communication in a healthy democracy.

DEFINING THE SUBSTANCE OF OUR STUDY

When we say we want to understand political ideology, what is it we want to understand? We will focus on three terms to orient our project: *ideology, political philosophy*, and *public motive* or *frame*. Our goal in defining these terms is not to be precise; rather, we hope that playing around with definitions of the terms will project a central core of substance that forms the heart of our project.

Ideology

The term *ideology* suffers from being loved too much in the twentieth century. Ideology is not simply a theoretical concept in political economy but has been wielded often in political discourse, particularly as a pejorative.[2] Etymologically, of course, the term derives from Greek roots meaning "the science of ideas." But in the current political discourse, its "-ology" root (meaning the science or study of . . .) has been left behind, and *ideology* has become a term of praxis. The notion of "ideo-," of ideas, has been retained, albeit with important emendations.

The most popular and widespread use of the term *ideology* in the twentieth century was in orthodox Marxism-Leninism. The term was a central concept in explaining false consciousness. In *The German Ideology*, Karl Marx and Friedrich Engels argued that the ruling classes were kept in power despite the facts of material analysis because of their mastery of ideology.[3] In a capitalist culture, they argued, the dominant institutions retain power through a commonly recognized and celebrated emphasis on values, fundamental understandings of how the world "really" works, and indoctrinated ideas of how the world "should" work. Ideology is propagated by those in power through normal daily activity. The schools, the family, and various cultural forms—including literature, media, music, and advertising—teach normality or the natural way things are. As we live daily life, employing the values, fundamental understandings, and judgments of the "good" and "desirable," those dimensions of ideology are reinforced and provide a greater control over our lives. Marx and Engels believed that ideology exercised its power by naturalizing (ideological structures seem the natural way things are), historicizing (ideological structures seem a result of the natural flow of history), and eternalizing (ideological structures employ notions like the "good" to identify the immutable truths of life that are as they are and cannot be otherwise). An effective deployment of ideology, Marx argued, gives a dominant regime or class maximum control with minimal conflict, and thus minimal effort at control (a notion familiar as *legitimacy*). Gramsci called this power for perpetuation of dominant social order *hegemony*.[4] In this tradition, it is through ideology that the masses become complicit in their imprisonment.

Orthodox Marxist-Leninist use of the term as pejorative sprang from their faith in historical materialism; that is, ideology is alienated from the material functioning of the world. It is, thus, false. It prolongs acceptance of the oppression of the working class. Its power can be broken only by historical-materialist analysis that reveals its falseness and its power to alienate the masses from the truth of their existence. The tradition believed that the power of ideology projected a false notion of "the world as it is" that enslaved the masses.

Ultimately, the orthodox vision of this tradition eroded. It became obvious to even the least sophisticated observer that the underlying processes of legitimation by praxis described and attributed power in this model were not simply characteristic of capitalist societies but described Marxist-Leninist societies as well. Furthermore, the essence of ideology is to *normalize* day-to-day social, political, economic, and cultural structures. The challenge in social change is to normalize alternative structures. This basic tenet of so-called *Neo-Marxism* embraced the power of ideology for change as well as hegemony and thus moved closer to the other dominant twentieth-century use of the term "ideology."

That second common use of ideology in the twentieth century acknowledged that typical ways of thinking about the world help to shape human action. Such an idea seems inherent in modernism and particularly in the Enlightenment. Descartes's *cogito ergo sum* assigns priority to thinking over materiality as a fundamental principle of reality. This assertion that the power to think and reason empowers human action entails recognition of the power of ideas. Although we will sometimes hear a pejorative version of this conception of ideology (e.g., "He is an ideologue!"), the basic notion that human action is guided and thus shaped by underlying beliefs and thought processes is widely accepted as a basic fact about society.

Many trace the beginnings of the use of the term *ideology* to the French Revolution. The ideologues of that revolution became a conscious intellectual class who viewed themselves as the shapers of revolutionary France. George Lichtheim has observed: "The 'ideologists' of the Institute were liberals who regarded freedom of thought and expression as the principal conquest of the Revolution. Their attitude was 'ideological' in the twofold sense: being concerned with ideas, and placing the satisfaction of 'ideal' aims (their own) ahead of the 'material' interests on which the post-revolutionary society rested."[5]

What differentiated the French Revolution from the American Revolution was simply a consciousness of the power that orchestrated ideas to reshape society. Consider these words by Thomas Jefferson in the Declaration of Independence: "When in the course of human events, it becomes necessary for one people to . . . assume among the powers of the earth, the separate and equal station to which the laws of nature and of nature's god entitle them, . . . We hold these truths to be self-evident, that all men are created equal, that they are endowed by their creator with certain unalienable rights." In these statements, the powers of naturalizing, historicizing, and eternalizing were clearly at work. Where the force of Jefferson's words was indeed a description of "the way the world is," the ideologues of the French Revolution presented their words as the way the world should be.

What the notion of ideology adds to the link between human thought and action is systemization. Beliefs, material expectations, notions of "good" and evil, and predilections to behavior are all interlocked in a fabric. The fabric holds its form. Change anywhere in the fabric is resisted by the systemic power of the form, but successful change then alters the systemic definition of the form, and thus changes reverberate through the total culture. The change becomes normalized.

Ideology captures the tendency of action to be relatively consistent over time and asserts that the consistency is founded in the processes of thought and rationalization that shape action. Furthermore, ideology provides the sense of centripetal force that shapes the actions of a society from integrated social processes rather than mimicry. The French ideologues took ideas as a category (a productive phenomenon for perception), studied the history, and asserted a science of ideas, and having created the study (note, ideologically true to its etymological origins), they thrust the power of ideas into the work of the revolution.

Ideology affirms that actions and their rationale are not isolated but woven into a broader fabric of understanding, anticipation, and value. We will see that real ideological work is rhetorical: it is performed in society within the communicative acts that constitute orientation, justification, and legitimation and that thus become the substance of political action.

Political Philosophy

The second term we will pursue to define our core pursuit is *political philosophy*. The term has meaning both as a formal study in political theory and in everyday political discourse. As a term referring to a mode of study, the generic *philosophy* carries several meanings elaborated in the more specific *political philosophy*. One prominent definition of the academic discipline of philosophy identifies its task as a search for first principles. This definition provides one central conceptualization of political philosophy: the search for the basic principles of government, the state, law, and authority, or even the search for the basic principles that justify institutions and coercive power in human affairs. Political philosophers trace theories of government, treating Plato and Aristotle among classical theorists and finding roots of modern democratic ideas in Thomas Hobbes, Jean Jacques Rousseau, John Locke, and other important philosophers of the Enlightenment. Such study seeks to relate political beliefs and practices to understandings of human nature and the origins of government.

Another common definition of a philosophy is the systematic exploration of the causes and reasons of a study. A political philosophy can be conceptualized as an understanding of the causes and reasons for political positions. This definition has taken us from political philosophy as a formal study of a universal human attribute—the joining together into communities in patterns of governance—into a method through which a variety of different political perspectives can be individually understood. The student of politics seeks the generative forces which manifest themselves in particular political actions. At the heart of Marxist analysis, for example, is a detailed theory that places the roots of political action in class interests. Alternative perspectives might trace political behavior to the need to develop methods to reconcile the pursuit of individual interests. For example, Madison's theory of the U.S. Constitution formulated in *The Federalist Papers* lays out a theory of coalitions interacting through politics to develop majorities to govern a democracy.[6] These perspectives can be taken to everyday politics to examine the causes and reasons particular actions emerge in political behavior. Thus, a theory is generated that explains the rise of the New Deal in the emerging interests of the American middle class in bringing more predictability and control to the economy.

In still a third definition, a philosophy is viewed as a systematic account of the assumptions and beliefs that underlie a complex of activity. Pursuit of a political philosophy can also be thought of as this search for the systematic unity of a political position. This type of study can locate assumptions about individual responsibility, about the ability of the market to reconcile individual interests without government interference, and beliefs about the threat excessive government poses to individual happiness in conservative political philosophy. Thus, opposition to government regulation and the lack of concern for market distortions can be united as pursuit of a single viewpoint on government's role.

As an academic study, political philosophy considers many aspects of political behavior: political economy, or the ways in which power interacts with the distribution of resources in a society; the appropriate balance between the powers of government legitimated as expressions of community will and the rights of individuals to resist that will; and the duties and responsibilities of government and citizen in relationship to each other.

Perhaps, in the technical sense, we are best to see political philosophy as a turning of the philosophers' purposes, tasks, and tools toward understanding power, governing, and the practices of the state. As an academic pursuit, the study of political philosophy values descriptive objectivity, tests its theories against political behavior, and generates debate about the texture of politics. Theoretically, such study stands above the performance of politics, seeking to inform public understanding of the process from the authority of academic method.

Our purpose here is neither to exhaustively define the concerns of formal political philosophy nor to provide an in-depth treatment of these issues. Rather, we point to the formal concern in political philosophy that characterizes particular academic interests. But, like its umbrella term *ideology*, *political philosophy* is also a vernacular term, occurring frequently in general discussion of politics. Political philosophy may be declared as an attribute of an office holder, a candidate, a political party, a political movement, or a segment of voters. Those engaged in political campaigning or in the processes of governance continually seek to characterize their own political philosophy or that of opponents. Negotiations to resolve political disputes often explore philosophical agreement as a method of reaching settlement. Political alliances and coalitions often develop characterizations of the political philosophy that unites adherents to their positions. Regardless of how broadly political philosophy is identified, the common assumptions are that (1) there exists an underlying set of beliefs, values, and assumptions that generate a consistency of political behavior, and (2) the consistency creates social or personal coherence.

The vernacular positions political philosophy as a more enduring notion than one's political stance toward a particular event or moment and as a more enduring notion than support for particular policies. This transcending of time then serves as a background to explain the reasons for, or the roots of, political responses to a given moment or particular policy positions. The positions of a candidate on the American health care system, its current problems and the solutions to those problems, can be attributed to the candidate's political philosophy about governmental responsibility for the welfare of citizens.

Viewed within this perspective of consistency across time, political philosophies may change, but not radically or often. Ronald Reagan may have touted his conversion from New Deal Democrat to free-market Republican, but the change was a gradual evolution in his thinking, with a clear directional drift. When George W. Bush charged that John Kerry held conflicting positions, he was implying that Kerry had no systematic political philosophy and thus could not be trusted to act from the pattern of reasoned adherence to a philosophy that Bush believed his constituents value.

In this meaning, political philosophy functions in two distinct ways. First of all, it stands as a summary understanding of a number of specific positions and policies. It removes the randomness from moment-to-moment governing, and thus provides coherence to political position. A sense for the candidate's political philosophy provides a more parsimonious catalog of his or her position on numerous issues. Bill Clinton's many policy positions and the other characteristics of his personality and public persona projected a candidate who appreciated the difficulties of ordinary Americans and sought to use the power of the presidency to solve problems that affected individual lives.

Political philosophy also functions, however, as a way for citizens to discuss the generative bases of specific political behaviors. The texture of everyday political discourse does not see political behavior as random. Rather, behaviors are seen as happening for definable and justifiable reasons. Those reasons are located in political philosophy. Ronald Reagan's support for deregulation of the economy could be found in his belief that a market economy in which entrepreneurs had maximum leeway to pursue profit promised the greatest economic return. So could his support for tax reductions. Many different policies of his administration could be attributed to this free-market philosophy.

In both of these functions, the use of political philosophy in the democratic vernacular permits all in the political system to transcend the isolated moment or the particular policy. Through political philosophy, interpretations of the past are tied to advocacy in the present and to predictions about the future. Politicians and their parties and other coalitions are expected to act consistent with political philosophy even if the vagaries of the moment may call for variation in response. Indeed, political philosophy has its power in the vernacular because it transforms the unpredictable into anticipated action. Regardless of particular vagaries of the economy, increases in unemployment, budget deficits, inflation, or innovation, Ronald Reagan could be predicted to favor free-market solutions.

One final observation about the vernacular use of political philosophy is important to understanding its role in politics: political philosophy may or may not be overtly articulated by those to whom a particular political philosophy is attributed. Those involved in politics may attempt to explain their philosophy: Reagan paid tribute to the free market, and George W. Bush declares his assumptions in a terminology of "values." However, political philosophy is not the product of individual messages, but of the complex of interpretation that involves the rich matrix of communication in political discourse. Commentators as well as opponents offer their interpretations of George W. Bush's political philosophy. Citizens offer their interpretations of the systematic beliefs that activate Bush. In this sense, political philosophy is a term of interpretation with which all of those involved in political processes conduct their organizing of the political landscape.

How does political philosophy relate to ideology? Like ideology, political philosophy has crossed from theory into vernacular. The meaning of political philosophy turns out to be very close to the second meaning of ideology. That second notion of ideology projects the faith that political actions are shaped by a core of beliefs, values, and assumptions about how the world works and the role of government in that working. Political philosophy is a shorthand term to describe this generative ideological framework and how it guides political actions.

There are other, more subtle differences in the use of the two terms. In the twentieth century, whereas ideology tended to emphasize the *limits* on the variety of differing perspectives within a culture, political philosophy emphasized the *possibilities* for choices that mark differences within a culture. Thus, communism, capitalism, and democracy are seen more as ideologies than political philosophies. In contrast, faith in the free market and belief in government responsibility to assure opportunity are viewed as attributes of political philosophy.

In addition, in usage, political philosophy emphasizes a conscious power to shape political action, ideology an unconscious power. In the vernacular, we believe that George W. Bush and John Kerry made choices in their lives that brought them to a political philosophy. We even believe that their philosophies may evolve, although we are suspicious if they radically alter them. But the assumptions of capitalism or the viability of protecting human volition through a defined set of rights are less disputed in our discourse, and thus are often described with a nomenclature of ideology rather than political philosophy. At extremes, this difference in meaning leads to opposite pejoratives: one controlled by ideology is condemned as an "ideologue," while one without a political philosophy is "without compass."

But differences can be exaggerated. We would emphasize the commonality of the terms: they stress the systematic coherence that generates and is generated in the discourse that accompanies political action.

Political Motive or Frame

In current usage, both ideology and political philosophy deny the isolation and randomness of political acts, and they share an underlying metaphysic that posits that ideas and thinking generate action. When it comes to studying political action, this metaphysic has been critiqued as mapping behavior within a theory of individual volition and thus being unnecessarily restrictive in characterizing social and political action. Influenced by the symbolic interactionists, this critique asserts that both ideology and political philosophy acquire their longevity and their ultimate influence by their articulation in socially constructed communication. Furthermore, to think of communication as neutral—as a mere conduit through which thought is transferred—ignores the powers of communication to evolve ideology and political philosophy.

We subscribe to this critique. We view political discourse as structured in motivational frameworks. Kenneth Burke has called these structures "motives" or "frames." We apply them specifically to political discourse and designate *political motives* or *political frames*. As structures applied to events as they occur, political motives are clusters of vocabulary and uses of that vocabulary that motivate political actors and actions.

Burke grounds his discussion of politics in the orientation that citizens assume toward the world around them. His rather lengthy discussion of ideology at the beginning of his book *Attitudes toward History* provides an efficient explanation of the functioning of ideology. Burke begins by describing how we orient ourselves to the world with a screen of judgment and an urge to act:

> In the face of anguish, injustice, disease, and death one adopts policies. One constructs his notion of the universe or history, and shapes attitudes in keeping. Be he poet or scientist, one defines the "human situation" as amply as his imagination permits; then, with this ample definition in mind, he singles out certain functions or relationships as either friendly or unfriendly. If they are deemed friendly, he prepares himself to welcome them; if they are deemed unfriendly, he weighs objective resistances against his own resources, to decide how far he can effectively go in combating them.[7]

To this point, Burke has described the origin of political action in judgments about the world rooted in a sense of anguish or injustice. He has not yet formed this orientation into politics, nor has he introduced the role of communication. He next does so. He describes the centrality of communication to the socialization of this orientation to the world. He describes how the rhetorical choices with which we shape our communication construct our sense of response, embody our orientation, and form our response into coordination with others to address the world together.

> "Action" by all means. But in a complex world, there are many kinds of action. Action requires programs—programs require vocabulary. To act wisely, in concert, we must use many words. If we use the wrong words, words that divide up

the field inadequately, we obey false cues. We must name the friendly or un-
friendly functions and relationships in such a way that we are able to do something about them. In naming them, we form our characters, since the names embody attitudes; and implicit in the attitudes there are the cues of behavior.[8]

Burke thus posits political behavior as coordinated in political communication. Communication in this view, however, is not random and not merely the
expression of individual political thought but a social interaction in which political response is negotiated and coordinated.

Burke next turns from describing process to describing clusters of language
choice and how they texture response.

Our philosophers, poets, and scientists act in the code of names by which they
simplify or interpret reality. These names shape our relations with our fellows.
They prepare us *for* some functions and *against* others, *for* or *against* the persons
representing these functions. The names go further: they suggest *how* you shall
be for or against. Call a man a villain, and you have the choice of either attacking or cringing. Call him mistaken, and you invite yourself to attempt setting him
right. Contemporary exasperations make us prefer the tragic (sometimes melo-
dramatic) names of "villain" and "hero" to the comic names of "tricked" and "intelligent." The choice must be weighed with reference to the results we would ob-
tain, and to the resistances involved.[9]

Burke labels these shared clusters of vocabulary employed in political action
frames of acceptance, "the more or less organized system of meanings by
which a thinking man gauges the historical situation and adopts a role with
relation to it."[10] Elsewhere he labels the frames *motives*:

But the question of motive brings us to the subject of communication, since motives are distinctly linguistic products. We discern situational patterns by means
of the particular vocabulary of the cultural group into which we are born. Our
minds, as linguistic products, are composed of concepts (verbally molded)
which select certain relationships as meaningful.[11]

Thus, Burke has constructed political action as performed in the learned vocabulary of our culturally accepted motivations. Elsewhere he recognizes that
this is what political theorists call "ideology," and he observes that this ideology is rhetorical in the traditional sense of that term.[12]

In a fundamental way, Burke reorients the way we think about communication in politics. He lays open the texture of communication, not as a window on the mind, but as an active arena of social response to the world in
which we live. The assertion and denial, the moralistic expression of how
things are and how they should be, the commitment to act, and the coordina-

tion of action together construct a framework of response. "The topic of rationalization," Burke notes, "has carried us beyond orientation proper into the *theory of motives*,"[13] and he adds into a process of rationalization. Thus, orientation (or the construal of context), rationalization (or the use of reason to sift understandings and responses), and motivation (or the reconciliation to values and identity that legitimizes and coordinates public response) are linked in the talk about the events of our lives. Burke studies this talk to understand human action.

A focus on political motives emphasizes the construction of the coherence of political action in communicative exchange. To motivate political action is to articulate a rationale for that action in common, familiar patterns that draw upon the culturally shared language practices and thus provide legitimacy for actions. The communication interaction is a negotiation in which the legitimacy of action is at stake, in which action may in fact become untenable, and thus political action itself is shaped in the interaction.

Politics is one of the grand arenas in which the public conducts the textured communication with which it responds to the events of the world through more or less rational processes. The grounding of these verbal responses in the texture of history, the past rationalizations and motivations for public action, provides the interest we have in public motives or frames for action. That these public motives are connected to culture and history lends them stability and leaves them as artifacts that we can study to understand the grounds of action. That they are recalled and shaped to ongoing events in political discussion is what leaves them open for our study.

LOCATING OUR STUDY

We share with other studies of ideology and political philosophy the observation that political action is accompanied by explanation and rationalization for public action. Like those studies, we take the discourse generated in such communication as our interest. Certain characteristics of political communication attract our attention. First, we are interested in the way in which the public orients its power to respond politically to events in a texture of communication about the nature of events and about the appropriate and effective response to them. We will view this orientation both as rationalization—the application of human reason to the events that surround the community—and as motivation—the reconciliation of response to values and identity. Second, we are interested in how political power is built through the power of this discourse to attract adherents. Thus, we view the communication as not only orienting with events but also orienting the public toward particular responses to those events. Third, we are interested in how this communication creates consistency across the body politic and across time in responding to events. There is a kind of glue spread liberally in this communication that binds people together in support of policies and that binds them with their political heritage to contribute to the sense of national identity and the legitimacy of action.

The term most appropriate for this critique of communication is *rhetorical*. For example, we look at the discourse following 9/11 and see choices of how to describe the events, how to construct their sequences and causes, how to relate them to our history, and how to marshal support for a societal response. All of these choices in language, image, perspective, and connection compose a fabric of coherent understanding that brings forth political action. The choices are neither random nor neutral but are embedded in a web of meaning, carrying perspectives that place any single response or event within a larger understanding of the past and the future. We are interested in laying open this process to see how coherence is created through rhetorical choices, emerges, and evolves into a shared public understanding that replaces the disorientation and individual explanations that followed the shock of airliners plowing into buildings. Thus, the substance of our study lies in that cluster of terms like *ideology, political philosophy*, and *political motive* that give shape to communication and mediate political action.

DEMOCRACY

Pondering the term *ideology* helped to define the object of our study. Now, pondering the term *democracy* will help to locate the purpose of our project. Etymologically, *democracy* is government by the people. In a pure democracy, all the people have access to the power of the state and participate in governing. Alas, we know democracy only in impure forms. *Direct democracy*, which we may define as government in which deliberation is by the people with choices of government action resting with the people, is extremely rare. Even those instances of direct democracy—ancient Athens comes to mind—defined citizenship with significant restrictions. Athenian democracy empowered only men who were heads of wealthy households. Women, children, people of modest means, and slaves were all excluded. Ironically, the celebrated Athenian democracy was only possible because the slavery of others provided the material freedom for the wealthy to participate in their democracy. The most cited example of direct democracy in American culture has been the New England town meeting. Confined in many ways to administrative tasks, the once-a-year town gatherings have been limited in the scope of tasks conducted by direct democracy. Between meetings, a small group has acted for the demos.

Representative democracy or a *republic* is another common form of democracy. In representative democracy, the people's power is to elect representatives who make the decisions for them. In fact, in the early American republic, *democracy* was often a pejorative term indicating mob rule, and the Roman republic was the model, rather than the Greek *agora*. Even today, with citizens' greater access to government, the government in the United States is a limited democracy. Moreover, because of the great disparities in power, many characterize government in the United States as an aristocracy or meritocracy in the Greek terminology. Citizenship is often reduced to the mere act of voting.

The other term often applied to democracy in the United States is *liberal democracy*. In liberal democracy, the power of representatives is restricted by defined freedoms. The Constitution, particularly the Bill of Rights, defines those restrictions in the system in the United States. Thus, majority rule has its limits defined by the essential founding document of the republic. The Declaration of Independence—which many identify as the founding document of the United States rather than the Constitution—was a document of liberal democracy. It described the sovereignty of the people—god-given—and the prerogatives of that sovereignty. It also set rights as a counterpoint, indeed a motivation, for the exercise of that sovereignty. When the Constitution was drafted in the republic's eleventh year, it differed from many of the state constitutions because it lacked a bill of rights that specified the limits of government and the domain of liberal rights. The ratification process required the promise of such a list as a price of approval and the first Congress passed the Bill of Rights.

Yet another variant of democracy is necessary to fix the nature of the system in the United States—*participatory democracy*. A generally broad term, *participatory democracy* suggests that the license granted to the representative is not absolute. There is a power reserved to the people to participate in their democracy. Thus, somehow, the representatives must listen to their constituents, must respond to their wishes and desires, and must answer to them. The processes by which this participation proceeds evolve and are quite informal. Animating participatory democracy is the very important notion of *legitimacy*. The term refers to the notion that an action is just and right.

So what does it mean in the United States to say that "the people rule"? Three principles mark the character of democracy captured in that phrase. First, the direction of government is in the hands of the people. Although such changes of direction are rare, changes that occurred with the elections of Abraham Lincoln, Franklin D. Roosevelt, and Ronald Reagan are within the power of elections in the United States. In other instances, powerful movements intent on changing the direction of government achieve limited influence, only to fail ultimately to take control. For example, in the late nineteenth century, farmers organized in the Midwest and South into a number of political parties, culminating in the early 1890s with the formation of the People's (Populist) Party. Nominating William Jennings Bryan for president in 1896, the Populists achieved influence within the Democratic Party. Their ideas eventually became a part of the agenda of Progressivism and had a profound effect on politics in the early twentieth century. To a lesser degree, any change in the political party in power alters those who shape government policy. Through the electoral process, the selection of leaders, and the organization of individuals and interests into coalitions, those out of power can work toward capturing a political party and through it appeal to voters to change government policy. The process of generating candidates, developing grassroots support, and assembling voting blocks creates the conditions of a negotiation between those in power, those who seek power, and the public that influences the direction of government.

Second, "the people rule" means that the legitimacy of government action is judged by popular response. Democracy in the United States is an efficient governing system because it depends heavily on nonviolent means of support. We persuade and cajole one another to share perspectives, images, and visions for the future. Today an industry has grown up designed to measure and document the legitimacy of governmental action through quantitative polling of public acceptance or rejection of leaders, candidates, policies, and actions. Policies without legitimacy and individuals without extensive public support fail. The war in Vietnam is the most salient example from the late twentieth century. Unpopular policies, even if supported by a majority, tear at the fabric of the society, taking a toll on the capacity of government to function normally. Ultimately, in the face of such opposition, governments change. Even though political polling provides a salient manifestation of this process, and elections a particular focus of vulnerability to governing power, the terms of legitimacy—the granting of the power to govern without resistance—are negotiated more fluidly in American democracy.

Third, "the people rule" means that the public possesses the power to affect government. In the American experience, democracy is widely understood as a government responsive to the will of the public. Government is conceived as being constituted "of the people, by the people, and for the people." Organs of government are in place specifically to respond to the public voice. For example, congressional offices have large staffs whose primary task is handling communication with constituents. Ultimately, elections are a negotiation of permission to govern. Victories at the polls grant legitimacy and the right to decision-making power. But that power is constrained by the demands of public voices.

Together these three dimensions constitute a scheme for evaluating the level of democracy in the United States. That evaluation varies from time to time as the government is more and less responsive to public sovereignty. To the degree the dimensions operate, however, the American government operates as a democracy.

Communication is an essential element of each of these dimensions. Changes in government are born in expressions of discontent that motivate change. Legitimacy is monitored, withheld, or granted in patterns of communication that are supportive or critical of government. Public effect on government depends on a stream of communication from public into government and on the response of government to that stream.

Ideology plays into this communication process because it provides a coherence that is presumed by these various dimensions of democracy. The very notion of a *direction* to government assumes a coherent path of action that is disciplined, shaped, and motivated by political philosophy. The negotiation of *legitimacy* requires a rhetoric that frames governmental action as just and right, and thus legitimate. And the communication of *public will* influences action as the public will is reconciled with governmental action in the coherent structures that are political motivations.

This viewpoint of democracy is sufficient to define our purpose at the moment. We have posited that the quality of governing we label democratic is present in varying degrees at different times in different societies. Our commitment in this project is to maximize that quality. We believe that a key factor in maximizing democracy is mastering the complex negotiation of immediate political action with coherent continuity provided by ideology. Our next task, therefore, is to define the link we assert here: that at its heart, democracy thrives when democratic action is linked to a relatively "stable" ideology. We do not view stable ideology as something that is forever enduring and essential, or as something that is forever fleeting and passing, but as something that holds for a period of time—give or take a few years within a twenty- to thirty-year period.

IDEOLOGY'S IMPORTANCE IF THE PEOPLE RULE

Any theory of democratic governance consistent with the definition that stresses the rule of the people will include an appeal to the consistency of beliefs, values, and assumptions that constitute the political culture. This consistency emerges with a stable ideology. To lay out this inherent role for ideology, we will examine democratic theory at two levels: (1) the democratic response to moments when government is asked to respond to events in the culture, and (2) the role of ideology in the bonds that coalesce the citizens of the culture into a political identity.

Ideology and Democratic Action

We begin by focusing on judgment and action that accomplish democratic character. A democratic system weaves together many moments of judgment and decision. Some decisions are made by leaders, some by citizens. Indeed, moments of democratic response are an intricate dance of gestures and discourse in which the exchanges of leaders and citizens accomplish the legitimacy of which we have spoken.

In moments of crisis, democratic leaders are charged with understanding the moment and selecting, proposing, and directing an appropriate response. Such choices involve complex political judgment. That such judgment begins with a particular understanding of the situation and the appropriate response to the situation seems obvious. Leaders gather information to help them understand the nature of the situation, what has happened, what its possible causes are, what the alternatives for response are. Judgment involves organizing this information into an understanding of the situation that justifies a choice of response. In addition, however, there is a judgment of political effect inherent in the choices. Who will be one's allies in implementing such a policy or response? Who will resist? What political price will be paid? How will the decision enhance the leader's political resources? How does the leader justify the choice to convince the public of the legitimacy of the choice? The responses to political action along these dimensions of judgment are negotiated in political discourse. Presidents, for example, introduce major policy initiatives in speeches that wrap the policies in ideological judgment as appropriate to, even demanded by, the circumstances of the situation. In acts of political theater, they surround themselves with supporters who endorse the action.

Such communicative acts seek legitimacy for the leader's choices. This legitimacy implies a complementary judgment by citizens: affirming the appropriateness and justice of the political action. The art of political rhetoric is the negotiating of this shared perspective of leader and public. Legitimacy reflects a shared judgment of appropriateness by the leader and the citizens grounded in a common perspective on what happened, on the values of the culture, and on a shared desire for outcomes from the political policy or response.

To illustrate, we return to an example we explored in chapter 1. In 1993, President Bill Clinton orchestrated a task force chaired by Hillary Rodham Clinton to produce a proposal for national health system reform. With the release of the task force's report, President Clinton began delivering speeches that explained the health-care crisis facing the country and the appropriateness of the Clinton plan in solving it. His rhetoric called upon the national ideology to garner support. He emphasized the significance of his proposal by identifying it with the actions of Franklin D. Roosevelt, waving a health-care guarantee card to recall the solidity of Social Security, established during Roosevelt's New Deal. Those who opposed his plan also called upon elements of the national ideology. The Health Insurance Association of America flooded the airwaves with advertisements, known as Harry and Louise commercials, which expressed basic American doubts about governmentally controlled programs. Louise ended each advertisement with a plaintive, "We can do better." The struggle that doomed the Clinton proposal played out with the invocation of conflicting selections from American ideology.[14]

Arrival at legitimate democratic action is facilitated if a consistency across time and place provides predictability in the response of citizens and leaders. Ideology is the source of such consistency. It is the web of meaning that gives any isolated action coherence and purpose. Political judgment is constructed from the understandings and beliefs about appropriate responses valued in the ideology. In their communications surrounding a policy or action, leaders call to the shared ideology of the culture as a basis for the legitimacy of the policy or action. Citizens respond with acceptance or rejection based on their judgment of the alignment of the action with that screen of ideology. Thus, the communicative exchange surrounding actions is crafted from the ideological material of the culture.

Citizens in a democratic culture perform other actions crafted by ideology. For the idea that "the people express their sovereignty in the selection of the leader" to be a viable principle, there must be consistency between promises by leaders during the campaign and at the time of their political action. Ideology expresses such consistency. Of course, we can say that leaders are selected by criteria other than a consistency of action—perhaps sheer charisma, a "he is like me" judgment, a "she knows what she is doing" judgment, or even a recognition of the superiority of the leader—but each of these bases implies a framework for judgment that is ideological. For example, a citizen's faith that a leader has the same essential qualities as the citizen requires a negotiation of which qualities will go into such a comparison and the dimensions along which such qualities are judged. Indeed, which is to guide our choice is itself an ideological question, debated intensely during democratic elections. What is the basis a citizen should use in selecting leaders? Do representative leaders act as more able surrogates in selecting action or as empowered extensions of the citizens' judgment? Is election a sign of merit or of some other special quality? And aren't such judgments of the values that shape democratic electoral choice basic values of a democratic system? Is choosing to engage in electoral politics at all an ideological decision?

By highlighting the consistency between a leader's promises and performance, we highlight a projection from the moment forward implied in the electorate's judgments. An election is also a referendum on a leader's past performance. Has the leader acted in ways consistent with public judgments? Did her judgment result in acceptably just action? Did he satisfactorily unite the public in support of his actions? The rich rhetorical exchange at any given moment in an election is about defining the consistencies and expectations that bind leader to public. The negotiation of this exchange takes place in the language of the ideology. Beliefs, values, and assumptions about government are the embodiments of people and the fabric of their judgments.

Finally, the very assumption that in a democracy the people select the direction of government assumes a consistency of action across time. Direction is, in fact, a tracing of actions with a consistency of some sort. What is the direction? What direction have we been pursuing? What direction should be pursued? These are questions filled with beliefs, values, and assumptions about the political culture. And once a direction is chosen, faithfulness to that choice requires reconciling actions in a particular moment to the overall direction chosen. Such historical and momentary choices require a discourse formed from the terms and patterns of the ideology.

Thus, inherent in democratic relationships of political action is a use of rhetorical discourse in a process of negotiation imbued with the elements of ideology or political philosophy. Choices of a moment—choices of leader or choices of action—inherently project consistency across time and across the culture. The texture of this projection is what we call ideology.

Ideology and the Bonds of Democracy

No other statement has so eloquently captured the nature of the bonds that compose democracy as Abraham Lincoln's in his first inaugural address: "Though passion may have strained, it must not break our bonds of affection. The mystic chords of memory, stretching from every battle-field and patriot grave to every living heart and hearthstone all over this broad land, will yet swell the chorus of the Union when again touched, as surely they will be, by the better angels of our nature." Using the language of mysticism, Lincoln called upon the power of the identification of citizens with the nation-state. He identified this bond with experience and with the constituted cultural memory that is history. He identified it with military sacrifice and projected the motivation for that sacrifice in the bond. To Lincoln, its power was his last hope to keep the union together.

The bond seems mystical, of course, only to the strictest of materialists. Social order and social forms are always constructed of such co-orientations. The relationships of trust and responsibility that link citizens with each other, with leaders, and with the past and future of a democracy are woven together in a complex pattern of communication. Burke has called this process "identification" or "consubstantiality." Consubstantiality is a co-orientation employing the political language that is shared by those in the community. Leaders justify action in terms of the political motives that carry power in the culture. The public responds, accepting or rejecting the legitimacy of the actions. Their mutual participation in the exchange creates the bonds of co-participation.

The founders of the American republic depended on Rousseau and Locke for a theory of social contract. The rhetoric that forms the social contract occurs across time as political exchange celebrates and critiques the rationale for action. In a modern constitutional system, a constitution becomes the means by which the terms of the social contract are committed to a document that when subscribed formally or by tacit acquiescence becomes the basis of the democratic state. Subsequent moments lived within the terms of the social contract reinscribe its terms on the activity of the society. Thus, the ideology of a political democracy gives form to the discourse of politics. The ability to participate in this discourse—to justify one's actions, support or opposition in the terms of the ideology—is the access to the democracy's power. Through this process, the past is formed and reformed into a shared memory that gives the present meaning and casts choices as essential steps in achieving an imagined future.

Thus, democratic theory gives great importance to ideology. Participation in the democratic system of the United States depends on the participants' ability to call upon the political motives that resonate in the American culture to justify and legitimate public action.

WHY DEMOCRACY FAVORS GOVERNANCE BY POLITICAL PHILOSOPHY

Despite the linkage of ideology to democratic theory, there are serious alternatives proposed as models for democratic political action. Inevitably public decisions about response to a moment involve three elements in some proportional mix: a decision maker or decision-making process, an assessment of the situation, and a sense of propriety and continuity.

Political idealists often take a position on political action emphasizing the first of these elements: the decision maker. This position has its classical statement in Plato's notion of the all-wise philosopher king, and its most vociferous defense in the Anglo world in the writings of Edmund Burke. Burke posited an extreme position on representative government. He believed the task of voters was to identify the wisest citizen in their midst and to empower that person to make decisions for them. Burke told the electors at Bristol: "Look, gentlemen, to the whole tenor of your member's conduct. Try whether his ambition or his avarice have justled him out of the straight line of duty; or whether that grand foe of the offices of active life, that master-vice in men of business,—a degenerate and inglorious sloth,—has made him flag and languish in his course. This is the object of our inquiry." The judgment of citizens on their representatives was to be a total judgment of the person. Certainly, Burke argued, the decisions of the representative can be examined, but in the context of a total examination of the person's character. "Let me say, with plainness," Burke proffered, "I who am no longer in a public character, that if by a fair, by an indulgent, by a gentlemanly behavior to our representatives, we do not give confidence to their minds, and a liberal scope to their understandings; if we do not permit our members to act upon a very enlarged view of things, we shall at length infallibly degrade our national representation into a confused and scuffling bustle of local agency."[15] Thus, the opinions of local citizens are subordinated to the minds and understandings of the elected leaders.

A second approach to democratic decision making, ephemeral pragmatism, emphasizes sensitivity to the character of the moment. The emphasis is on a technical and thorough understanding of a situation, and the belief is that the guidance of pragmatism will dictate to the wise leader the proper response in that moment. The classic example of a leader attuned to his moment is Winston Churchill's leadership of Great Britain during World War II. Churchill had a long history of warning of the Nazi threat and urging British preparedness prior to the invasion of France in 1939. Calling him to the Prime Ministry was a matching of political philosophy to moment. During the war, Churchill maneuvered the Allies to British interests at each turn of the wartime situation. With the war over, Churchill and his party were defeated in the elections.

Before we proceed to why democracy mandates a sufficient role for political philosophy in decision making, we must first observe that malignancy is possible under any mix of these three elements in decision making. Critics of the United States' involvement in Iraq have argued that the decision to embark on war with that nation's government was the result of political philosophy trumping national intelligence.[16] This argument suggests that political philosophy became so dominant in the decision-making process that it lost its sensitivity to national intelligence and instead designed intelligence to fit its needs for proof. Conversely, during the 2004 presidential campaign, Senator John Kerry was perceived by many as rudderless. He was said to "flip-flop" on the issues depending on the circumstances of the moment. The decision on Iraq is an example of the malignancy of political philosophy. The changing positions of Kerry provide an example of the malignancy of ephemeral pragmatism. So the argument that we make is not for a need to attend to political philosophy alone. We acknowledge the importance of a proper balance among the elements that compose democratic decisions: wise decision makers, accurately understanding situations, and responding to them with the consistency that political philosophy affords. Our argument at the moment is for the importance of the third element in this mix: a sense of propriety and continuity.

We disagree with Edmund Burke that citizens of a democracy ought to forfeit judgment in individual moments to their wise leaders. Likewise we disagree that wise political action is only triangulated by slavish attention to the vagaries of individual moments. The creation of a living, engaged democracy requires a process where democratic theory infuses the conversations and judgments that form the substance of governing. When the process of democracy is reduced to a battle of sound bites and shallow images, decision making is reduced to little more than options based on self-interest. People are unable to critically generate or evaluate choices with any sense of coherence with the past or possibilities for the future. In contrast, when democracy includes processes and practices that bring political philosophy into the conversation, democratic decisions are able to reflect a consensus on what is collectively understood to be the best, the good, the most just course of action.

First, political philosophy better frames government as a coherent response to its era. What political philosophy contributes that ephemeral pragmatism cannot is what we might call *spread*, that is, seeing historical patterns even in specific moments. The result is that public decisions transcend the particular moment. We see a realization of the need to characterize eras in our politics. The passing of the Cold War at the close of the twentieth century represented not only an end to an era but also an unsure inquiry into the nature of the new era. We can easily see that Franklin D. Roosevelt's concerns and the coalition he built to address them were supplanted by the growth of conservatism in the late twentieth century. Although the politicians' declaration of "new eras" may often be exaggerated and function more as political slogan than careful analysis, a democracy does see itself in a time defined by the challenges that mark the era.

The United States today lives in a time of terrorism. This is not a statement about any single moment in space and time, but about the era. Democratic decision making must have the patience to locate the nature of the time in which we live and develop a coherent response to it. The continuity of such response is dependent on a rich, discursive process that guides leaders and grants their actions legitimacy because of their consistency with public understandings of the demands of the time. Furthermore, political philosophy not only gathers time into the development of the understanding of an era, but it also places that era into relationship with the historical character of the democratic culture. The United States has commitments that transcend the era, including commitments to human rights and to international cooperation. Political philosophy applies the resistance to arbitrary action that requires the Bush administration to justify preemptive war doctrine as a precursor to its use. In this way, political cultures have a kind of character that Edmund Burke might well recognize, and action is contextualized into that character by political philosophy.

The second reason democracy demands political philosophy is its importance in enabling citizens to transcend selfish interests in favor of public good. In *The Federalist Papers*, No. 10, Madison presented his theory of coalition of interests. He pondered the dominant judgment of the day that democracy could only work in small communities. Madison located the secret of the American Constitution in its mechanisms that encouraged the clustering and subordination of small, confined interests to the general good that would be required to build majorities. He emphasized the processes of compromise and consensus building, the identification of common interests that any single group in a large, fragmented nation-state would need to master to achieve influence. To Madison, these processes were not a kind of intuited magic but were achieved in the hard work of governing. Political philosophy emerges from this search for commonality and identification among interests, and its presence in decision making is an important recognition of the need to shape decisions to attain the support of the developed coalition.

Third, democracy requires political philosophy because the evolution of political philosophy permits the evolution of a democratic culture. The users of motion picture or television cameras know that one of the secrets of cinematography is the restricted movement in the camera carriage that smoothes out changes in the perspective of shots. The stark distraction of jerky motion is diminished if there is a means of resistance to change of perspective. In political culture, political philosophy is that medium of resistance. The rhetorical work to justify changes of policy in terms of the political philosophy of the culture evolves that philosophy. The engagement, reflection, evaluation, and consensus that characterize this process enable the political culture to grow and mature. For example, Franklin D. Roosevelt declared in his first inaugural address: "Action in this image and to this end is feasible under the form of government which we have inherited from our ancestors. Our Constitution is so simple and practical that it is possible always to meet extraordinary needs by changes in emphasis and arrangement without loss of essential form."[17] In doing so, Roosevelt was folding the dramatic changes he was to bring about in the constitutional ideology of American political culture. He praised the Constitution for its flexibility at a time when it would need to be so. Roosevelt used other strategies, including identifying America's historical pioneering spirit, which responded to challenges with innovation and dedication. Many have called Roosevelt's first inaugural address a conservative speech for radical times. The characterization, far from being surprising, is what we would expect in a democracy—the declaration of consistency in a time for change. By identifying the elements of American political philosophy that he would uphold and defend, Roosevelt permitted evolution of that philosophy consistent with those identified principles.

Fourth, democracy requires political philosophy as a rhetorical framework for contextualizing action. A political actor can announce an action or a policy, but democracy requires that the actor contextualize the policy, justify it, and orient it to the character of the political culture. Political actors must find the language, images, and interpretations to connect significant decisions with their context in political philosophy. Political philosophy is the reservoir, holding meaning, myth, images, and hopes in relationship to each other in patterns that give a firm basis to political action. The democratic imperative that leaders justify and thus seek the legitimation of their actions compels political actors to avail themselves of political philosophy as a context for action. The motivations for public action authorized by the political culture are the basic sources of argument and image in which political leaders find the justification for their actions.

Fifth, political philosophy facilitates legitimacy of action. Most importantly, political philosophy provides the rationale for rightness and justice that is the basis of legitimacy. Placing decisions within the framework of the political philosophy rationalizes them. In addition, however, the identification that is established in the co-celebration of the political philosophy as the action is justified strengthens the bonds between leaders and citizens and delivers the legitimacy of action. In short, justificatory communication about public action is an exercise that strengthens the bonds between government and citizenry even as it enfolds specific actions in legitimacy.

Finally, democracy favors political philosophy because of the virtues of stability. We have already discussed the ways in which justifying an action in terms of political philosophy provides a sense of continuity to an action. That same continuity projects stability of action. Stability is particularly important in international relations. Predictability of action permits coordination of nations' foreign policies. Political philosophy provides a framework for rationale that projects consistency even as policy may evolve. This function of stable ideology not only facilitates domestic legitimacy but also the consistency of action to improve international relations.

For these many reasons, ideology facilitates democracy. A democracy in which leaders justify actions in terms of political philosophy and in which the citizenry shares the sense of rightness and justice captured in the justification is a stable and productive culture. The energy of the culture is devoted to advancing the purposes and well-being of the culture, rather than struggling to maintain the viability of governance.

DIMENSIONS OF THE IDEOLOGICAL FUNCTION IN A DEMOCRACY

We have argued in this chapter for the importance of a rich rhetorical component in a well-functioning democracy. Such rhetoric weaves the action of governmental leaders into the beliefs, values, and motivations of the culture. The substantive embodiment of this rhetoric, the structure which the rhetoric calls upon for its powers of explanation and motivation, is the ideology, the political philosophy, of the culture. In this last section of the chapter, we seek only to highlight the functions that this rhetorical texture of contextualization serves in a well-functioning democracy. As we have placed ideology into democratic theory and as we have identified the advantages that a democracy gains from a rich rhetoric of justification and legitimation, the functions which democracy achieves have emerged.

The first function is what we might call the development of a *consensus in the definition of a situation*. Political discourse in a moment of action draws from the vocabulary and the perspective of ideology to present an understanding of the situation. This is the realistic function of rhetoric, the power that discourse has to communicate a particular perspective on events. In a functioning democracy, the public shares the experience of events. The novelty of the events provides a sense of dislocation that triggers a discursive search for understanding. As leaders, those in positions of power offer their interpretations, often competing explanations of the events. Each interpretation draws upon a particular facet of the culture's ideology to orient the events to the motivations and commitments of the ideology. As events proceed, some characterizations seem to more accurately map the events than do others. The discourse notes this relative success or failure. Through the exchanges of democratic discussion, a consensus evolves around a characterization of the events. At some point, a consensus begins to build legitimacy for a particular action.

A recollection of the responses to the events of September 11, 2001, will reflect this process in action. The typical initial response to the collision of an airliner with the World Trade Center's north tower was that a horrible accident had occurred. The orientation of concern was for those caught in the inferno in lower Manhattan. But the second airliner flying into the south tower rendered this explanation untenable. Two such "accidents" do not happen on the same sunny morning. Now, these seemed much more likely to be intentional acts. The flight of the third airliner into the Pentagon confirmed this understanding. Calculated acts of destruction against the peace and tranquility of American life were underway. Still uncertain was who had organized these events and how well-organized they were, and most importantly, how the society should respond to disasters of this magnitude.

The communication coming from the national media and spreading into the discussions in front of television monitors began to sort through responses based on the nature of the events. Some suggested that these were criminal acts and looked forward to the identification of the perpetrators and the planners of the seemingly coordinated attacks, and bringing them to justice through the powerful American judicial system. Others immediately labeled the events acts of war, as dramatic moments that would alter lives, compared them with Pearl Harbor, and began to develop expectations of military response to these enemies of the United States. America's leaders initially expressed the same confusion of response even as they began to identify the responsible party: Osama bin Laden and the terrorist group al Qaeda. Here was a shadowy group that we may have heard about in the past, but now their actions turned the attention of our response directly to them. Most of our knowledge of them came through our leaders. But that these events were orchestrated by a sinister figure who had declared war on American society emerged as a description of the situation that made sense to a large proportion of the public. Using the ideology of war, the administration prepared a military response and began to set aside the kinds of protections of the rights of citizens built into the American criminal justice system.

We have moved gradually into the second function that ideology plays in democratic action: *legitimacy*. For the process in which an understanding began to emerge from the public discourse that surrounded the unfolding events also began to identify the appropriate governmental response. President Bush identified the Taliban government of Afghanistan as the target of American military action because it had hosted the training bases of the al Qaeda organization and continued to shield bin Laden. Administration rhetoric proposed, however, a complex response even beyond the military action. The clear need to attack the al Qaeda organization was shaped into a broad approach: to identify and seize their finances, to locate and destroy their sleeper cells, and to alter the methods of controlling foreign nationals. As the activities and strategies of al Qaeda came into full view, a sense for the appropriateness of specific actions emerged. Debate and resistance to some actions remained, based on their erosion of civil and human rights, but that debate ultimately could not prevail against the sense of legitimacy expressed in the name "USA Patriot Act" that was attached to legislation increasing the power of government over the individual lives of Americans. <Security> developed as an ideograph justifying all sorts of actions that only months before would have been unthinkable.[18] The ideograph was institutionalized in a Department of Homeland Security that sought to organize resistance to terrorists within U.S. borders. The administration used color codes and warnings to express the dangers of further attacks by an unseen enemy in communities across America. Governmental actions spread, and the ideology of security and the first responsibility of government to protect its citizens was woven into a legitimacy of response.

The legitimacy function of discourse ties the description of the situation to a third function of ideology, the *moralization of action*. Legitimacy is not only a judgment of the power of a response to remedy a problem, but also a judgment of rightness and justice. When the administration demanded increased power of surveillance and restrictions on individual liberties, a debate followed that weighed security against other rights. Thus, the moral issue was enjoined. Sometimes that issue was diverted into legal questions. Did those captured in Afghanistan and held at Guantanamo Bay, Cuba, enjoy the rights of hostiles under the Geneva agreements? Did these agreements, defining the morality of war, apply to this situation? Within the consensus of the legitimacy of war, the morality and thus legitimacy of these actions were questioned. Nevertheless, the horror of the September 11 attacks also demanded revenge against the terrorists who launched an attack on American civilians.

Emerging from the discourse that framed the events of September 11 and shaped public response was a fourth function of ideology, an *identification* of the citizenry with the national project and with the leaders of that project. Patriotism grew. Celebrations of first responders and their dedication to the community followed. They were accompanied by celebrations of the determined quality of New Yorkers to continue to live their lives. The character of Americans was celebrated as well in a determination to carry the battle to the enemy. In short, the basis of American unity was located and celebrated. Approval ratings for President Bush soared as he asserted the legitimacy of the actions of the American government. By November 2001, Bush basked in a job approval rating of 89 percent, with 90 percent support for the military action in Afghanistan.[19] The character and the shared commitment of the American democracy formed around the rhetoric that declared our commitment and our dedication to response.

An important resource for this declaration of unified action was entailed in the fifth function of ideology, the *placement of these events into our history*.

Kenneth Burke has termed this function the management of permanence and change. These two terms are dialectical terms, that is, any given response to be successful must contain elements of both permanence and change. They must be seated in the character that endures across time and binds the political culture together. They must also adapt to the novelty of each situation and address the situation appropriately as it evolves. The references to Pearl Harbor as a metaphor for the attacks invoked an analogous historical moment as a context for the current moment. In his address of September 20, 2001, President Bush placed the attack in the long line of attacks on Americans through the nation's history, and then he explained how this war was different. The history made our route familiar; the uniqueness prepared us for differences.

Ideology provides the language and the strategies to shape political action rhetorically into the history and values of the culture. It is this rhetorical resource of ideology that plays out in these five dimensions to weave individual political decisions into the overall framework of American democratic governance. As we proceed to discuss strategies through which we can identify and incorporate ideology into political motivation, we seek to perform these functions in political rhetoric.

A CITIZENSHIP OF IDEOLOGY

In this chapter, we have identified the substance and purposes behind our inquiry into political ideology and democracy. We have argued that political discourse drawing from its attendant ideology is a necessary part of fundamental democratic processes. Implied are a set of rhetorical skills that define public situations, justify choices of response to them, construct a consensus supporting such actions, and direct the successful implementation of those decisions. These rhetorical skills are required of both leaders and citizens. The power of a skilled rhetor as a democratic leader is well documented. A leader's power in individual moments is founded in the leader's ability to use political motives to frame the actions that he or she believes are required to meet the contingencies of the moment. For citizens in a democracy, the responsibilities for participation in government require a complementary facility in working with the beliefs, values, and assumptions that identify the heart of the democracy. Citizens must cast their judgment in elections, and in support of policies in between elections. Further, we have a rich history of citizens joining together to articulate shared interests and values that demand the attention and support of their representatives. A democratic leader who cannot marshal the support of his or her constituency will find implementing a policy difficult if not impossible.

Thus, public conversation is an ongoing process. Leaders and citizens communicate in a rich mixture of opinion about the world we share. The essence of our interest in ideology is our belief that democracy exists only when the communicative exchange among people includes a wide-ranging dialogue about the fundamental values and perspectives that give meaning to our shared political culture. Political philosophy and ideology are essential components in our capacity to make judgments about political behavior and action.

NOTES

1. Michael Calvin McGee, "The 'Ideograph': A Link between Rhetoric and Ideology," *Quarterly Journal of Speech* 66 (1980): 1–16.
2. Several sources have contributed to the understanding of ideology reflected in this section: Terry Eagleton, *Ideology: An Introduction* (London: Verso, 1991); McGee, "The Ideograph"; George Lichtheim, "The Concept of Ideology," *History and Theory* 4 (1964–1965): 164–95; Karl Mannheim, *Ideology and Utopia*, trans. Louis Wirth and Edward Shils (1929; New York: Harcourt, Brace, and World, 1966); Goeran Therborn, *The Ideology of Power and the Power of Ideology* (London: Verso, 1980); Hans Barth, *Truth and Ideology*, trans. Frederic Lilge (1961; Berkeley: University of California Press, 1976); Karl Marx and Friedrich Engels, *The German Ideology*; Terry Eagleton, *Marx* (New York: Routledge, 1999); James Arnt Aune, *Rhetoric and Marxism* (Boulder, Colo.: Westview Press, 1994); Raymond Williams, *Marxism and Literature* (Oxford: Oxford University Press, 1977); Ian Adams, *The Logic of Political Belief: A Philosophical Analysis of Ideology* (Savage, Md.: Barnes and Noble Books, 1989).
3. Marx and Engels, *The German Ideology*, 1–2.
4. Antonio Gramsci, *Selections from the Prison Notebooks of Antonio Gramsci*, ed. and trans. Quintin Hoare and Geoffrey Nowell Smith (New York: International Publishers, 1972).
5. Lichtheim, "The Concept of Ideology," 165–66.
6. James Madison, *The Federalist Papers*, No. 10.
7. Kenneth Burke, *Attitudes toward History*, 3rd ed. (1937; Berkeley: University of California Press, 1984), 3–4.
8. Burke, *Attitudes toward History*, 4.
9. Burke, *Attitudes toward History*, 4–5
10. Burke, *Attitudes toward History*, 5
11. Kenneth Burke, *Permanence and Change: An Anatomy of Purpose*, 3rd ed. (1935; Berkeley: University of California Press, 1984), 35.
12. Kenneth Burke, *A Rhetoric of Motives* (1950; Berkeley: University of California Press, 1969), 103.
13. Burke, *Permanence and Change*, 18, emphasis in original.
14. The analysis here is from Haynes Johnson and David S. Broder, *System: The American Way of Politics at the Breaking Point* (Boston: Little, Brown, 1996).

15. Edmund Burke, "An Extract from Speech at Bristol Previous to the Election," *Selected Prose of Edmund Burke*, ed. Philip Magnus, www.ourcivilisation.com/ smartboard/shop/burkee/extracts/chap8.htm (September 24, 2004).

16. See, for example, Ralph Martire, Editorial, *Chicago Sun-Times*, October 9, 2004, 23.

17. Franklin D. Roosevelt, "First Inaugural Address" (March 4, 1933), www .americanrhetoric.com/speeches/fdrfirstinaugural.html (September 24, 2004).

18. McGee uses the convention of angle brackets to indicate that a word is an ideograph.

19. Richard Morin and Claudia Deane, "In Poll, Americans Back Bush," *Washington Post*, November 8, 2001, A11.

3

Political Positions and American Politics

In the opening chapter, we described the current political scene in the United States in a state of confused disorientation. We tracked many of the failures evident in governmental processes to the rhetorical practices that separate political messages from their ideological grounding. After considering the contributions of ideological grounding to a well-functioning democracy, we are ready to develop our recommendations to reconnect communication and ideology.

In one sense, our advice is obvious: political communication needs to reconnect to ideology as it motivates political action. But that process is difficult enough that an example of such revitalization will serve our objective well. We will focus on the revitalization of the political positions—radical, liberal, conservative, reactionary—as a key rhetorical tool to perform the democratic functions of ideology. We described the confusion of political positions in chapter 1. We believe that the most important move to overcome this confusion is to see the connection between ideology and action as a dimension of rhetorical strategy as well as a dimension of political policy. Indeed, the task of connecting ideology and political action is a rhetorical task embodied in messages of political motivation. In this and the next chapters, we develop a method of using rhetorical analysis to replace policy identification in working with political positions. We propose a system for identifying political positions and generating consistent messages from a shared political philosophy.

There are several points of analysis that taken together allow us to align particular rhetorical strategies with particular political philosophies. At each point, proponents of the different political positions call upon strategies typical of their position to connect their underlying political philosophy with the action they advocate. We argue that because of the potential of rhetorical strategies to consistently connect ideology and action, they are ultimately a more stable indicator of political position than ephemeral policy statements. By orienting political communication to those strategic choices, political philosophies can again become a fruitful symbol performing the democratic functions of ideology.

Political positions are among the most common symbols of political ideology. In the chaotic confusion of the current political culture, traditional policy definitions of political positions are of little value because people who call themselves liberals and conservatives betray the policy expectations for those respective political positions. George W. Bush, for example, calls himself a conservative. Traditional conservative ideology calls for a diminished role for government. As Ronald Reagan would say: We've got to get the government off our backs. However, Bush, who began his presidency with a balanced budget, runs annual deficits of $500–600 billion. He calls for federal action to monitor public schools and limit abortion and same-sex marriage. These are hardly actions identified with traditional anti-governmental conservatism.

In this chapter, we explore adapting the political positions that have been valuable in defining the range of American political opinion. The American political system has always been a rich mosaic of political philosophies. American democracy has been contested ground. We want to explore the roots of the political positions that have offered organization to that mosaic. We find the matrix of those positions in two attitudes: the attitude toward change and the attitude toward the structure of current institutions. We see the political positions and the symbols that come to stand for them in political communication as again potentially useful intermediaries between ideology and political action. In chapter 4, we develop an alternative approach to the analysis of political communication that reintegrates politics and ideology through the rhetorical strategies of the four major political positions.

A HISTORY OF AMERICAN POLITICAL POSITIONS

Within Western democracies, multiple worldviews compete for political power.[1] Clinton Rossiter characterizes this multiplicity in his system of political positions. Rossiter posits a circle with seven categories: revolutionary radicalism, radicalism, liberalism, conservativism, standpattism, reaction, revolutionary reaction.[2] We are uncomfortable with Rossiter's system. By inserting "standpattism," he designates conservatism as the middle and most desirable position. Further, he adds a revolutionary category to both radicalism and reaction. Our problem with this is that we see no clear line to differentiate the revolutionary impulse, because violence is seldom advocated but often a result of the divisions that follow advocacy and resistance to extreme change. This system, by adding three new positions, significantly changes the spirit of the four basic terms and appears more difficult to apply. Our approach focuses on the four basic political positions—reactionary, conservative, liberal, and radical—that have marked political dispute in the West generally and in the United States particularly. These four political positions not only organize current political dispute, but they do so with historical linkages to the Western political tradition.

The Origins of Modern Political Positions

Late in the eighteenth century, groups with different views of the world and corresponding political philosophies emerged to define the four major political positions. Each group responded differently to the same circumstances and to each other.

Strains of liberalism came from political theorists Thomas Hobbes, John Locke, and John Stuart Mill. Hobbes viewed the fundamental liberal principle as freedom and posited that restrictions on liberty must be justified. He accepted this principle as the beginning of liberal political theory. Hobbes was at best a qualified liberal, because he argued that drastic limitations on liberty *can* be justified. Locke not only advocated the fundamental liberal principle but added that justified limitations on liberty must be infrequent and modest. In 1790, John Stuart Mill introduced utilitarianism as he discussed the relationship between action and social values. Mill's utilitarianism is expressed commonly as a political philosophy seeking the "greatest good" for the "greatest number." This became central to the liberal position.[3]

As liberalism grew, it took slightly different forms in different countries. In England, liberalism emphasized religious toleration, government by consent, and personal and economic freedom. In France, liberalism was more identified with democracy and secularism. In the United States, liberalism often combined an emphasis on personal liberty with a wariness of the social impact of capitalism.

Radical ideology was born out of an extreme dedication to liberalism. Radicals emphasizing freedom sought fundamental change in the structure of society that they viewed as inherently restricting liberal freedoms. Some people see the beginning of radicalism in the American Revolution, while others point to its origin in the excesses of the French Revolution. Radicals took the idea of individual freedom and carried it much further than liberals, including a willingness to sacrifice social stability to achieve those freedoms. Radicals also opposed the conservative tendency to tie individual rights to property rights.[4]

Conservatism was first articulated by Edmund Burke reacting to the excesses of the French Revolution. As mentioned in chapter 2, Burke advised that society should place the wisest person in leadership. He accepted that a social contract bound society to traditional values and only allowed gradual change. Conservatism, also, was less a political philosophy than a way of life or an attitude toward change. Burke believed change should be a rational process, not based on speculation, metaphysics, or theory.

The reactionary political position grew out of the French Revolution. Some people wanted to restore the conditions of a previous period. They were essentially extreme conservatives, very reluctant to change. They favored the old aristocracy over the middle and working classes even though at times they favored the conservative bourgeoisie. As elitists, reactionaries supported strong, even authoritarian governments, and they opposed democratic and parliamentary forms.

The political positions grew as a way for political figures of the late eighteenth century to work through the realities of their time in terms of the emerging Enlightenment ideas of the purposes and functions of government. The emerging theory of freedom of the individual founded on limitations on the state met the terror of the French Revolution. The result was a lively debate on both sides of the Atlantic that adapted political philosophy on one hand and circumstances in France on the other to the particular characteristics of each political culture. The political positions became touchstones around which particular positions in the debate coalesced. Today, the political positions carry that same potential to facilitate an adaptation to concrete circumstances and philosophical possibility if they can be appropriated with the interpretation of public events.

Differing Attitudes toward Change in Political Positions

The four major political positions emerged to mark the variety of political responses to the same situation. They continue to organize political debate through their differing attitudes toward change. Each position assumes that as circumstances change, a behavior should be modified appropriately. At a given point in time, each of the four political positions has a different perception of the appropriate response to the situation. We can illustrate this with a tale of freeway driving. Imagine that while you are driving to the office in the morning, you hear an announcement on the radio that there is a three-car crash narrowing the freeway to one lane about five miles ahead, directly in your intended path. Most people under these circumstances would expect to be in a major traffic slowdown ahead and would think that now was the time to take an alternative route if one was available. More conservative drivers would recall all those days when this freeway, even with crashes, had moved them on their way and would be hesitant to find an alternative way. More liberal drivers would assess the circumstances, recognize the impediment in their way, and actively seek an alternative route.

Differing attitudes toward change define the four political positions. The *reactionary's* attitude is that behavior or policies have been changed much more rapidly than circumstances justify. So the reactionary favors a dramatic change returning to a proven older policy or way of doing things. The *conservative's* attitude is that changes in behavior and policies have moved faster than circumstances justify, so the conservative only wants a more measured pace of change or to hold the line. In contrast, the *liberal's* attitude is that policies have lagged behind what changing circumstances warrant, so the liberal wants to speed up policy change. Finally, the *radical's* attitude is that behavior and policies have lagged far behind changing circumstances, so the radical wants to make dramatic changes toward new policies.

The important thing to note is that these are four different responses to the same set of circumstances based on four different perceptions. In rhetorical terms, these different attitudes toward change become four different lenses through which people view the world and translate their interpretation of the world into political action. A problem, however, is that the definitions are not concrete when making sense of the chaos in culture through the lens of political ideology, which makes it consistently difficult to draw lines among the positions on the basis of ephemeral issues.

An Example of Ideological Diversity and Issue Instability: The Role of the Federal Government

No issue is more long lasting in American politics than the role of the federal government. Since the beginning of American government in the late eighteenth century, political positions and even the established political parties have differed in favoring or opposing a strong federal involvement in private life. The longevity of the issue illustrates the constancy of ideological diversity in American politics, but it also illustrates the instability that results from trying to apply policy definitions to political positions.

Government under the U.S. Constitution began in the dispute over the power of a central government. The Constitutional Convention was organized on the urgings of five states whose representatives, motivated by frustrations with the weakness of central government under the Articles of Confederation, convened in Annapolis, Maryland, and recommended a convention to revise the Articles. What emerged, of course, was the Constitution giving new powers to the national government. Whether that power was excessive was one of the key issues of the several state conventions that ratified the Constitution. In those debates, proponents of the Constitution embraced the label *Federalists*, thus leaving their opponents with the obstructionist label *Anti-Federalists*.

Who should be labeled the *conservatives* and who should be labeled the *radicals* in this debate has been a matter of considerable dispute among historians. On the one hand, the ideology of the American Revolution had resisted an established British governmental structure remote from the citizenry. The first act of rebellion was the empowering of Committees of Safety that wielded considerable governmental power in localities. In this sense, the radicalism of the American Revolution favored the position of the Anti-Federalists. This interpretation paints the Federalists as conservative—seeking to maintain a measure of central control in a national government, an idea that was very European. On the other hand, the Revolution itself was one of those traumatic events that may well have reversed the sense of the status quo. From this perspective, independence established the weak central government as the status quo. The Federalists embraced the Constitution as a radical idea in a time of the weak government of the Articles. Madison's federalism was portrayed as a bold new republican experiment in government. Notable also among the issues that developed during the ratification debate was the promise to adopt a Bill of Rights that made the new government into a guarantor of liberal rights. In this interpretation, the Federalists assumed the position of the left, with the Anti-Federalists conservatively defending the relatively weak government of the Articles of Confederation.

The Constitution did not envision political parties, but in the early years of the republic they developed along the fault line that marked the attitudes toward a strong federal government. As the presidential election of 1800 approached, Thomas Jefferson, the liberal Anti-Federalist candidate, embraced change and argued that the best government was the one closest to the people. After all, the people had just successfully fought a war for their freedom from the British king, so Jefferson was suspicious of a strong central government. Jefferson saw a strong central government as a threat to liberties, and he resisted the slide toward increasing governmental power that had been initiated by the Constitution. In contrast, John Adams, the conservative Federalist incumbent who was defeated in the election, defended the Constitutional claim for a stronger central government as necessary to maintain order and promote the national interest. Thus, in the early republic, conservatives embraced the need for a strong central government while liberals resisted such power. In the first half of the nineteenth century, champions of federal power such as Henry Clay's National Republicans, later the Whig Party, promoted the role of the government in internal improvements and urged governmental action to protect developing American industry. Their opponents in Andrew Jackson's Democratic Party resisted the federal role.

The general democratic tendencies that emerged with the election of Jackson in 1828 and the active movement for radical reform that grew in the 1830s and 1840s began to erode the stability of this viewpoint on government. The national debate began to revolve around slavery and emancipation. The founding of the Republican Party in the 1850s began to realign Jefferson's Democratic Party as the conservative party opposing federal involvement on slavery, as the defender of traditional society, and opponent of the dramatic change that emancipation would bring. The Republican Party attracted former Whigs but with commitments to use federal power to limit the spread of slavery and even emancipate the slaves to establish their economic and civil rights. As the Civil War approached, southern conservatives stressed states' rights and resisted the increasing interest of the federal government in spreading democratic civil rights. Lincoln, as a child of Henry Clay's "American System," promoted government involvement in the economy. He was thus a reluctant liberal, but the Emancipation Proclamation became the instrument through which the abolitionists and reformers began to see the strong federal government as a benign power. The party of Jefferson and Jackson became the bastion of conservatism and the party of Lincoln the center of liberalism.

The next great shock to political positions came from the effects of industrialization and the growth of the factory economy. After the end of the reconstruction period following the Civil War, the Republicans presided over the growth of the power of the industrialists, and their political power unloosed the public land giveaways and political corruption generated by the support for railroads. The Democratic Party embraced the reforms of the Populists and William Jennings Bryan. The Populists gave rise to the Progressives in the early twentieth century. The left, thinking that they could use the federal government to weaken big business, passed laws such as the Sherman Anti-Trust Act in 1890, which allowed government to break up large monopolistic businesses. The left also tried to help those who were less fortunate with laws such as the Clayton Anti-Trust Act in 1914, which legalized labor unions, and the progressive income tax in 1913, which tried to reduce inequality by taxing upper incomes at a higher rate than lower incomes. The Republicans' attitude and response (with the notable exception of Theodore Roosevelt) was to oppose these bills and the expanded role for government in the economy. This reorientation became dominant with Franklin D. Roosevelt's New Deal. This last view of the role of the federal government— Democrats favoring a stronger and Republicans a weaker role—has become conventional wisdom for our day. In fact, the left and right have maintained these positions for sixty to eighty years.

Yet, even as politicians continue to mouth the conventional wisdom, today we are experiencing another left and right reversal of the federal government's role. Beginning in the 1950s, and with the Nixon presidency, but mainly in the 1980s and 2000s with Reagan and Bush, Republican behavior has changed to increase the role the federal government plays in a number of areas, and Democrats have called for decreasing it in a number of areas. Nixon, for example, implemented government wage and price controls and initiated a low-level guaranteed family income. Ronald Reagan, while talking about "getting the government off our backs," ran up budget deficits five to six times larger than those of Jimmy Carter, his Democratic predecessor. George W. Bush doubled and tripled Reagan's deficits to $500–600 billion. All three presidents, Nixon, Reagan, and Bush, acted to increase the role of government while arguing that government should be smaller. And in the last quarter-century on issues such as abortion, gay marriage, and media content, social conservatives have projected an increased role for the federal government in regulating the lives of citizens.

On the political left, we have seen signs of radicals backing away from big government as the answer to societal problems. In the 1960s, a group of social movements referred to as the "New Left" advanced an abstract vision for the future based on the philosophy of anarchy rather than the traditional communist or socialist blueprint for society. In the 1970s and 1980s, radicals began to coalesce around the environment and the need for a smaller, sustainable scale for life. They argued that America's waste and greed were ruining the environment, and if citizens wanted to pass on a quality way of life to their children, they needed to cut back on their use of energy and other resources. Radicals see large business and government as counter-productive and as mainly responsible for environmental problems. Returning to the central concern for individual rights, the left has opposed the use of government as a means of imposing particular values.

Bill Clinton and George W. Bush continued the reversal of positions about the federal government's role. Clinton, contrary to earlier Democratic policies, stressed balancing the budget and freer trade in the form of NAFTA. Moreover, Clinton appropriated the Republicans' issue of "family values." George W. Bush supported government restrictions on abortion, promoted a large military, and appropriated the Democrats' issue of "education," doing so by involving the federal government in enforcing standards. The Bush foreign policy made it very clear that Republicans no longer favored a weak federal government, but instead supported active promotion of American values in other nations.

The rhythm of political reversals on the role of government makes the practice of defining political positions through this issue problematic. The trading of issues and symbols that characterizes the current political role reversal is part of a larger societal change—a paradigm shift in societal thought. With dramatic changes in thought, traditional definitions of the political positions based on the role of government break down.

AN ATTITUDINAL DEFINITION OF POLITICAL POSITIONS

The reversal of positions on the issues surrounding the role of government illustrates the tendency of the political positions to become unstable when they are dissociated from a grounding ideology. At the level of issues, such reversals are easily discovered through history. Political positions become more stable, however, if we begin to examine the consistency with which proponents of the positions articulate the ideological grounding. To understand this more consistent pattern, we return to the notion that the political positions reflect differing attitudes toward change. We label this a *functional approach* to political positions.

The strength of a functional approach is that the political stance is identified from the attitudes toward the structure and context of the policy *at a given point in time*. The functions of the political positions are established by examining a given piece of political discourse for its acceptance or rejection of the structure of the policy and drift of policy on the issue over time. These two functions, structure and drift, allow us to identify the relationship between policy and ideology framed in the discourse.

Structure. All policies are implemented through an institutional structure that may be unified or a loose combination of elements that have evolved over time. The structure defines common assumptions and procedures that shape public implementation of a policy. The political middle accepts this structure and defines its attitudes toward change within it, while the political extremes reject some important element of the structure.

The structure of medical care in the United States, for example, is a combination of individual responsibility, limited pro bono services, insurance usually provided through employers, and government-supported services such as clinics, Medicare, and Medicaid. The political middle, conservatives and liberals, accept the elements of this structure and seek modifications within it. The political extremes reject the structure: radicals reject individual responsibility for care and reactionaries reject the role played by government.

Drift: Over a period of thirty to fifty years, policy changes on a particular issue are not random but move in a perceivable direction. The political left—radical and liberal—accepts and would accelerate policy change in that direction, and the political right—reactionary and conservative—rejects and would inhibit or reverse it. For example, within domestic policy from the turn of the twentieth century to the 1970s, the direction for change was toward a greater role for the federal government in economic policy. This included a movement for government to see that medical care was available to citizens, regardless of their economic well-being. At times, specific policies adopted were designed to stop the drift. These efforts were usually short lived, only slowing down the drift for a period, not eliminating it.

Across specific policy debates, the attitude toward structure and drift generates stands on specific policies, and marks a consistency in political positions. This level of attitude transcends particular policies and issues, thus providing a more stable definition of the political positions. When arranged by their acceptance or rejection of the structure and drift on a specific policy issue, the four positions may be explained as follows:

A *reactionary* rejects both the structure and drift of present policy.
A *conservative* accepts the policy structure but rejects the drift of the policy.
A *liberal* accepts both structure and drift of a given policy.
A *radical* rejects an element of the structure and accepts the drift of a policy.

The political definitions can also be presented visually as points along a political continuum, as shown in figure 3.1.

These functional definitions connect more basic attitudes and interpretational strategies to a given stand on a political issue at a given point in time. This approach recognizes that people and political parties can take inconsistent stands on different issues and at different points in time. The stability in the definitions results from the identification of political position with interpretational attitudes grounding more deeply than the vagaries of the moment.

An Example: Unemployment Compensation

The functional approach can be illustrated by applying the definitions to the United States' policy of unemployment compensation. First, we must identify the structure and the drift of the policy.

Structure. The Social Security Act established the policy of unemployment compensation in 1935. Each state has since passed laws implementing the federal policy. Under the current structure, involuntarily unemployed workers receive payments, reduced from their earned wage, for thirteen weeks. The policy is implemented through an insurance system where employers pay into a fund in boom times to compensate for the stresses on the fund in slack economic times. This insurance pool is then supplemented by federal appro-

Drift of History

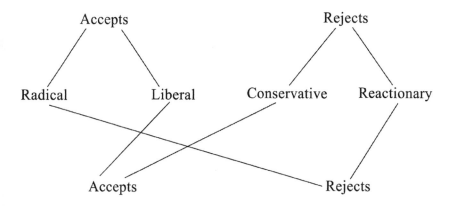

Structure of Current System

Figure 3.1. The Functional System of Political Positions

priations and partial payment by former employers during the period of unemployment.

Drift. The drift for the policy, since it was established in 1935, has been to increase the amount of the payment, extend the period of the payment as levels of unemployment increase, and increase the ability of the legislature and/or executive to modify conditions of compensation in response to state and local economic conditions.

Having described the structure and the drift for the policy of unemployment compensation, we can identify the four political positions through the functional approach. The issue of unemployment compensation arises frequently in periods of recession. In the debate over extensions of unemployment compensation, the voices of the four political positions are heard.

Reactionaries reject both the structure and drift. The most extreme reactionaries will not only reject the compulsory nature of the government plan but will also reject altogether the concept of unemployment compensation. They argue that people should receive wages only when they work. They view the entire policy as immoral and believe the government should rescind it and return to a policy of only rewarding hard work. In fact, they argue, policies such as unemployment compensation have contributed to the moral decline of the nation.

Conservatives accept the structure but reject the drift. They accept the structure that people should receive some compensation when they are unemployed through no fault of their own. However, they oppose increasing the amount and period of compensation because they believe it rewards laziness and will reduce the incentive to seek new work. They favor reducing the size and scope of unemployment compensation programs.

Liberals accept both the structure and drift. They accept the idea of unemployment compensation as well as adjusting both the level of benefit and the length of unemployment covered by compensation. They take these positions because they want to provide a cushion for individuals unemployed for reasons beyond their control, reducing the personal impact of losing a job on individuals and their families. Further, they see the program as a tool of government fiscal policy, offsetting the reduced demand resulting from the lost job, and thus useful to slow economic decline, prevent additional unemployment, and hasten recovery from the economic recession.

Radicals reject the structure but accept the drift. They reject the elements of the policy that prevent a person from automatically qualifying for compensation when they are unemployed, and the assumption that the response to unemployment should be to address the loss of income rather than the loss of a job. But they support the trend toward the government's taking greater responsibility for improving the unemployment system. Actually, they favor the government playing an even greater role, because they generally favor a guaranteed annual income or an income floor beneath which no person would be allowed to drop. They also may support guarantees of employment either through the employer or, in the extreme, through government ownership of production.

CONCLUSION

We have seen that the four political positions have a long history of serving as symbols to define the diversity of democratic politics. When political positions are connected only to issues, they have an instability that leads to their failure to serve as coalescing symbols at certain periods in history. The result is confusion in political orientation and the failure of the positions to serve their role in restoring stability to politics.

The functional approach we have outlined in this chapter is a general system for identifying the policy stands appropriate to each political position. Identification of structure and drift on any particular policy provides a scheme that organizes the range of policy stands on an issue. The specific content of structure and drift varies over time as various issues pass into and out of public dispute, but the relationship of the political positions to each other provides a stability to political debate. At the heart of that stability is the attitude of the various positions to change, its threats, and its promises. Our argument is that connecting political positions more thoroughly with ideology provides a more fruitful role for political positions in democratic processes. Political positions can become intermediaries between ideology and policy and more fruitfully organize political processes of change. In the next chapter, we examine the rhetorical strategies typical of the political positions as a way to illuminate the connections of political positions with ideology.

NOTES

1. Kenneth Burke, *The Rhetoric of Religion: Studies in Logology* (1961; Berkeley: University of California Press, 1970). Political ideology is different in Western and Eastern cultures. In the West, ideology is deeply rooted in the fall/redemption model of Christianity, where people continually experience the cycle of rebirth. In Eastern cultures, ideology is rooted in the perennial now. In this project, we are considering language choices in the Western perspective.

2. Clinton Rossiter, *Conservatism in America* (New York: Vintage Books, 1962), 11–14.

3. Gerald F. Gaus and Shane D. Courtland, "Liberalism," in *The Stanford Encyclopedia of Philosophy*, ed. Edward N. Zalta, http://plato.stanford.edu/archives/win2003/entries/liberalism/ (January 8, 2005); Gerald F. Gaus, *Justificatory Liberalism: An Essay on Epistemology and Political Theory* (New York: Oxford University Press, 1996), 162–6; Michael Ayers, *Locke: Ideas and Things* (New York: Routledge, 1999); Thomas Hobbes, *Leviathan*, ed. Michael Oakeshott (Oxford: Blackwell, 1948); John Stuart Mill, *Utilitarianism and Other Essays*, ed. Alan Ryan (New York: Viking, 1987). For more discussion, see Richard Rorty, *Philosophy and Social Hope* (New York: Penguin Books, 1999).

4. For further description, definition, and discussion of the four political positions—liberal, radical, conservative, reactionary—see Bernard L. Brock, "A Definition of Four Political Positions and a Description of Their Rhetorical Characteristics" (Ph.D. diss., Northwestern University, Evanston, Ill., 1965).

4

Rhetorical Strategies and the
Four Political Positions

We have argued that one of the keys to a more effective democratic political system is a fuller articulation of political motivation by connecting political discourse with its ideological roots. Doing so, we believe, requires a greater awareness and utilization of rhetorical strategies that achieve this richness in political discourse. Chapter 3 focused on the four major political positions to illustrate the way differing positions in the political debate have potential to become symbols of ideology to enhance democratic political action. That chapter addressed the ambiguity and instability that results from attempts to define political positions on the basis of policies. We argued for a functional approach to identifying positions, locating the differences among the political positions in their attitude toward change rather than in specific, ephemeral policy stands. In this chapter, we expand the system for revitalizing political positions.

Our study of the four major political positions identifies distinct rhetorical strategies that each position adopts to connect political action to its underlying philosophy. Those strategies combined with the functional definitions provide a stable language for each political position. We also explore commonalities in strategy among the political positions that open strategic opportunities to form the coalitions so necessary to effective governmental action.

In discussing the rhetorical strategies, we depend heavily on the framework and terminology of Kenneth Burke. Burke's philosophy of communication is particularly attuned to understanding the relationship between language acts and their underlying generative frameworks. Burke is a contextualist, a member of the intellectual movement that views communication as the fundamental human activity. Contextualists see the essential act of communication in the negotiation of interpretations in order to come to terms with the events that define public life. Burke not only informs understanding of this role for communication but also provides a vocabulary that illuminates the process.[1]

We begin by examining Burke's viewpoint on the role of communication in human affairs, then proceed to explore the language strategies with which proponents of the various political positions interpret the world around them to motivate political action.

TYING IDEOLOGY TO ACTION: RHETORIC AS INTERPRETATION

Political discourse contributes to a general public discussion of the public events that mark day-to-day lives. Citizens, leaders, and political commentators offer disparate interpretations of the texture, meaning, and significance of these events, and the appropriate responses to them. The dialectical process of thick communicative exchange that greets significant political events develops what Burke calls *the definition of the situation.*[2] Rhetorical interpretations, Burke argues, are strategic, stylized responses to events and reflect a person's ideology. "These strategies size up situations, name their structure and outstanding ingredients, and name them in a way that contains an attitude toward them."[3] Rhetorical strategies are strategic not only in this sense, but also because they have appeal; that is, they seek to socialize response, to bring others in the rhetor's social group to agreement with the interpretation in the process Burke calls *identification.*[4] In the communicative process, the public evolves a jointly developed understanding of the situation and the appropriate response to it. The diversity of voices that participate in that coming to terms with the moment enriches the developing consensus. For leaders, successful appeal and the subsequent identification imbues their actions with that feeling of appropriateness that we call *legitimacy.*

Burke finds the basis of identification in several dimensions of rhetorical strategy. Above all, he sees such identification involving what he calls *the dialectic of permanence and change.* This dialectic stresses that every moment is both unique and like other moments. Rhetors' interpretations orient the public response to the commonly held experiences of the community and to the community memory held in its history. One of the dimensions of this community experience and memory is ideology. "We discern situational patterns," he argues, "by means of the particular vocabulary of the cultural group into which we are born."[5] Ideology is a shared vocabulary that allows the development of understanding and legitimate response to proceed. "Ideology is," Burke writes, "but a kind of rhetoric (since the ideas are so related that they have in them, either explicitly or implicitly, inducements to some social and political choices rather than others)."[6] Burke also stresses the link between understanding and response.[7] For Burke, to motivate action is to offer a definition of the situation within which our cultural memory identifies a particular response as appropriate. Thus, selecting a vocabulary of war to frame 9/11, to see the twin towers of the World Trade Center in an invoked analogy to Pearl Harbor, begins the process of motivating war as a response. Burke calls this process the development of *substance*.[8] Substance, he points out, is literally what stands under an interpretation. That strategy inevitably generates from substance accomplishes the linkage of policy to ideology.

Obviously, Burke views communication as much more than the expression of individual thoughts. He views communicative acts as themselves productive, locating the significance and meaning of discussed events and issues in our history and our culture, and producing a socialized understanding that legitimizes coordinated response. Rhetorical strategies place particular messages into this thick context of history and culture to guide action.

Burke's aptly named book *A Grammar of Motives* is a consideration of the strategies that link discourse with its substance. The volume therefore presents a rich vocabulary with which we can map interpretive strategies that link ideology and political action. Our next task is to work with the political positions and to identify characteristic strategies that each position employs.

LANGUAGE CHOICES OF THE FOUR POLITICAL POSITIONS

In *A Grammar of Motives*, Burke introduces his vocabulary for motivational analysis, *the pentad*: "In a rounded statement about motives, you must have some word that names the *act* (names what takes place, in thought or deed), and another that names the *scene* (the background of the act, the situation in which it occurred); also, you must indicate what person or kind of person (*agent*) performed the act, what means or instruments he used (*agency*), and the *purpose*."[9] Burke calls the pentad a "calculus" for understanding motivation and substance.[10] Thus, the pentad is a tool that helps us understand how words and clusters of words acquire characteristic form and function to create particular interpretations of situations that link ideology to action.

Burke points to two characteristics of a "rounded statement about motives" that we must also map if we are to understand the variety of strategies for defining a situation. First, he notes that such statements emphasize one term over others. This observation forms the heart of his project in *A Grammar of Motives* because this emphasis on a single term is shared by all rhetoric generated from a single philosophy or ideology. The philosophies that associate with the emphasis on the various elements of the pentad are: scene = materialism; agent = idealism; purpose = mysticism; and agency = pragmatism.[11]

Second, he notes that rounded statements feature one of the terms but entail all the terms; the variety of motivations are generated as the other terms are shaped by the character of the central term. Burke uses the term *ratios* for the structural variations that explain the power of central terms to shape other terms.[12] A text may emphasize the character of the scene, and consequently the act, purpose, agency, and agent attain their character from the scene. Or the text may feature agent, and consequently the act, scene, agency, and purpose attain their character from the agent. Imagine, for example, a person who enters a convenience store, stashes a loaf of bread in his coat, and walks out without paying. In reporting this incident, one observer says: "I know the kind of person he is and this does not surprise me. He is a criminal, doomed to a life of crime. We will be safe only when people like him are off the streets." Another observer says: "Unemployment is so high right now, leaving many people without the means to feed their families. There is little surprise that he was driven to this. Something needs to be done to address the hunger that results from this economic recession." A third comments: "It was theft, clear and simple. Setting out to take something for nothing has become too common a pursuit in our society." A fourth offers: "An economy that creates such extremes of wealth and poverty invites the poor to redress the imbalance. Taking the bread is a small, necessary way to respond to the poverty that seems inevitable in this economy." In order, these different statements about the same act emphasize the agent, scene, purpose, and agency. The act—from theft to feeding his family to protest—takes its color from the central term. The character of the thief—from irredeemable to loving parent—likewise is dependent on the character of the central term. The nature of the appropriate response differs: punishment to fiscal policy to societal regeneration to rejection of the capitalist system. We will soon see that the strategies employed to interpret the situation are characteristic of the conservative, the liberal, the reactionary, and the radical.

MOTIVATING POLITICAL ACTION: LANGUAGE STRATEGIES TO DEFINE THE SITUATION

The combination of a grammar that allows discernment of the variety of rhetorical strategy and the tie to the underlying philosophy that generates the strategy provides us a method for proceeding to identify the rhetorical characteristics of the discourse of the various political positions. Those who define public situations from the perspective of each political position, consciously or unconsciously, shape their attitudes toward change and structure into an emphasis on a different element of the pentad. The common strategies with which rounded statements of motive are articulated become key elements of political motivation.

Reactionaries' major rhetorical strategy is to argue from purpose or principle, which Burke argues is characteristic of the philosophy of mysticism. Consider George W. Bush's opening remarks at his April 4, 2004, press conference. He began: "Before I take your questions, let me speak with the American people about the situation in Iraq." He followed with a brief description that consisted of a listing of the people instigating the violence. These people were identified by their purpose: "Although these instigations of violence come from different factions, they share common goals." Thus, Bush presented the continuing hostilities in Iraq as a test of wills. The enemy doubted American purpose; the United States must make war to demonstrate the commitment to its ideals. He defended American action by citing American purpose: it is not imperialism but liberation. In the face of questions about failures in Iraq, he pleaded for patience by drawing a parallel to the American Revolution, which he said was similar because both had "achieving freedom" as their goal. The roots of his position in a mystic philosophy emerged in his expressed belief that "freedom is the deepest need of every human soul." Near the end of the press conference, in a digression on an unrelated question, he summarized the roots of American war: "I also have this belief, strong belief, that freedom is not this country's gift to the world; freedom is the Almighty's gift to every man and woman in this world. And as the greatest power on the face of the Earth, we have an obligation to help the spread of freedom."[13]

Bush's statements illustrate the reactionaries' interpretation of the world. They are rooted in a mystically apprehended American purpose and the principle of demonstrating a will to act toward that purpose. Like his sorting of those that are for us and those that are against us shortly after September 11, 2001, those who make war against the United States do so for malignant purpose. Iraq as a scene of war is defined as the battleground between purposes. Thus, the agents, the scene, and the act are all defined in their ratio from purpose. Reactionary discourse presents given or natural laws—apprehended principles and/or purposes—as governing life and society. Reactionaries view the difficulties of the world as arising from the turning away from these essential truths. Their solution is to bring behavior and public policy back in line with original laws, principles, and purposes.

Robert Bork's *Slouching toward Gomorrah* is another example of reactionary ideology drawn upon in rhetorical strategy to motivate a political agenda. Bork argued that American society is deteriorating as it moves away from the traditional values and principles that made the nation great, and America's only hope is to return to these values.[14] Other people who generally illustrate reactionary rhetoric are Jerry Falwell and Pat Robertson of the Christian Coalition. White Supremacists use even more extreme reactionary rhetoric.

Conservatives primarily argue from the character of the individual or agent, a typical perspective of the philosophy of idealism. Consider Ronald Reagan's 1984 State of the Union Address. He opened by addressing the American people personally through Congress: "You and I have had some honest and open differences in the years past. But they didn't keep us from joining hands in bipartisan cooperation to stop a long decline that had drained this nation's spirit and eroded its health." By talking about "you and I" and "joining hands," Reagan is looking at the world through the perspective of agent. It was his initiative with the assistance of those he addressed that explained the American renaissance. He proceeded to chronicle the range of problems improved through his first term. Those narratives of improvement featured individual stories of accomplishment by citizens released from government burdens and overcoming difficulty to succeed. It was Reagan who added the citizen-heroes in the balcony as a feature of the State of the Union Address. His domestic policy promised to end regulation and increase opportunities for such individual success:

> The problems we're overcoming are not the heritage of one person, party, or even one generation. It's just the tendency of government to grow, for practices and programs to become the nearest thing to eternal life we'll ever see on this Earth. And there's always that well-intentioned chorus of voices saying, "With a little more power and a little more money, we could do so much for the people."

As Reagan closed the address, he worked the agent-purpose ratio, expressing purpose in the image of the reputation of his time in the eyes of a later time: "Let us be sure that those who come after will say of us in our time, that in our time we did everything that could be done. We finished the race."[15]

Even though at times he leaned toward the reactionary position, Reagan generally spoke as a conservative, and this speech illustrates his conservative rhetoric. The speech viewed the world as individuals reacting to each other and defining the texture of politics. The speech was sprinkled with traditionally derived values and the philosophy of idealism—the faith in the power of individual reason to solve problems. Reagan, like conservatives, described a world in which people control their own destinies and in which good people make good decisions. Problems arise when people make the wrong decisions.

If the right person is in a leadership position, all problems can be solved, and Reagan was that leader. This language is reflected in the well-known phrases "get the government off my back" and liberalism is like "throwing money at problems." The political maxims leave an image of a person carrying the government around and another person sprinkling money around like grass seed.

America's cultural tradition of the Western frontier, with its trappers, ranchers, and farmers, and today's business people and soldiers illustrate this conservative ideal of a person controlling his or her destiny. Horatio Alger's "Rugged Individual" and today's astronauts are examples of the conservative's ideal individual. The Western cowboy and the detective as hero also are popular icons of American conservatism. These images permeate conservative discourse.

Liberals' major rhetorical strategy argues from the situation or scene, a strategy grounded in the philosophy of materialism. Consider Bill Clinton's 1999 State of the Union Address. Clinton opened the address by describing his view of the state of the union: "Tonight I stand before you to report that America has created the longest peacetime economic expansion in our history — with nearly 18 million new jobs, wages rising at more than twice the rate of inflation, the highest homeownership in history, the smallest welfare rolls in 30 years — and the lowest peacetime unemployment since 1957." With his careful delineation of the statistics of success, Clinton provided what Burke would label a focus on scene. He continued his strategy when elaborating on the budget: "For the first time in three decades, the budget is balanced. From a deficit of $290 billion in 1992, we had a surplus of $70 billion last year and now we are on course for budget surpluses for the next 25 years." As Clinton shifted from the domestic to the foreign scene, he revealed the same strategy but at a different level as he discussed the South Asian financial crisis:

> This is the most serious financial crisis in half a century. To meet it, the United States and other nations have reduced interest rates and strengthened the International Monetary Fund. And while the turmoil is not over, we have worked very hard with other nations to contain it.
>
> At the same time, we have to continue to work on the long-term project, building a global financial system for the 21st century that promotes prosperity and tames the cycles of boom and bust that has engulfed so much of Asia.

Clinton closed the address by projecting the scene into the future:

> A hundred years from tonight, another American president will stand in this place to report on the State of the Union. He — or she — will — will look back — he or she will look back on a 21st century shaped in so many ways by the decisions we

make here and now. So let it be said of us then that we were thinking not only of our time, but of their time; that we reached as high as our ideals; that we put aside our divisions and found a new hour of healing and hopefulness; that we joined together to serve and strengthen the land we love.[16]

In presidential politics, the Democrats most frequently represent the liberal position, and Clinton illustrated liberal rhetorical strategies. Liberals describe circumstances as the major force influencing behavior, so one must decide how to intelligently adjust policies to the situation or scene. This is why they are very descriptive in their strategies and present numerous facts and examples. This is why calls for change are rooted in detailed descriptions of the current situation. Liberals orchestrate solutions to problems, maximizing positive and minimizing negative impact on society.

Although his wavering from liberal strategies on issues contributed to the current ideological chaos, even President Clinton's compromising approach to leadership and zig-zagging rhetorical style provide a good example of liberals' use of circumstances. Clinton's rhetoric focused on varied circumstances and the seemingly contradictory positions they required. For example, he supported a balanced budget as well as increased funding for Medicare and college loans, all supported with appropriate descriptions of motivating circumstances.

Radicals primarily argue from agency or the structure of a problem or event, thus calling upon a pragmatic philosophy. They believe that the means of delivery or structure of any policy or process is central to its effectiveness. Consider the 2004 Nader for President website as an example of radical rhetorical strategies. Nader's language choices revealed a radical stand on the issue of health care by favoring a program of universal care:

> The United States spends far more on health care than any other country in the world, but ranks only 37th in the overall quality of health care it provides, according to the World Health Organization. The U.S. is the only industrialized country that does not provide universal health care. More than 44.3 million Americans have no health insurance, and tens of millions more are underinsured. Private corporations pay less than 20% of health costs. Thus, even if you have insurance, you may not be able to afford the care you need, and some treatments may not be covered at all.

Nader's description focused on the health-care delivery system and its failure. Nader called for structural changes: "The Nader Campaign supports a single-payer health care plan that replaces for-profit, investor-owned health care and removes the private health insurance industry (full Medicare for all)." Agency became the driving force of Nader's argument as he opposed company control and favored a government program for all citizens. Nader's language choices also revealed a radical position on energy. He called for the United States to move from coal, oil, and nuclear toward newer and cleaner sources of energy. Nader also opposed the invasion of Iraq, favored withdrawal from Iraq, and supported spending some of the money saved on education:

> The quagmire of the Iraq war and occupation could have been averted and needs to be ended expeditiously, replacing US forces with a UN peacekeeping force, prompt supervised elections and humanitarian assistance before we sink deeper into this occupation, with more U.S. casualties, huge financial costs, and diminished US security around and from the Islamic world. The faulty and fabricated rationale for war has the US in a quagmire. Already more than $155 billion has been spent, adding to huge Bush deficits, when critical needs are not being met at home. We should not be mired in the occupation of Iraq risking further upheavals when our infrastructure, schools and health care are deteriorating. Four years of free public college and university tuition for all students could be paid for by $155 billion.[17]

Nader would radically change United States priorities in many areas, qualifying him as a radical. He characteristically advocates structural changes, which situate him within the philosophy of pragmatism. Radicals believe that principles, intentions, and circumstances need to be translated into more tangible instruments of change to be effective. In the 2004 campaign, Nader employed this strategy as he argued that corporate money controlled both the Republican and Democratic Parties.

Karl Marx's *Communist Manifesto* and Stokely Carmichael's *Black Power* are good examples of radical philosophy and rhetorical strategy. These two intellectuals took account of the structure and policies of society and recommended sweeping change—revolution. Green Peace and radical feminists such as Starhawk also illustrate radical rhetoric. The radical looks at language choices and other rhetorical strategies to account for and change the existing structures and policies of society.

The tendency of the four political positions to interpret situations with different emphases and constructions provides us with a method for understanding the ideological basis for political discourse. Descriptions of the world and the legitimate public actions in response to it are formed from the attitudinal consensuses that define the different political positions. Furthermore, discourse that substitutes rounded statements of motives for reductions to slogans provides a basis for the choices and identifications that facilitate the effectiveness of political democracy.

MOTIVATING POLITICAL CHANGE:
LINKING INTERPRETATION TO ACTION

In chapter 3, we tied political positions to characteristic attitudes toward change. If we are correct in indicating this key difference, we should find variation in linguistic strategies to motivate change, just as we have found differences in strategies to interpret situations. Indeed, the ideological link between interpretation of situations and the legitimacy of political action is carved in divergent language strategies that transform the emphases on particular terms of Burke's pentad into rhetorical motivation for change.

In earlier work, Brock has called Burke's framework for rhetorical motivation *the dramatistic process.*[18] The process unites five moments (five isolated phases of a psychologically or sociologically balanced process):

1. *Order.* Change begins, Burke argues, against the background of the orderliness of the world. The rhetoric that motivates change projects a vision of that order.
2. *Disorder or Pollution.* As the rhetoric focuses on current conditions, it motivates by contrasting the current world to the vision of the orderly. Thus, the disorder in the current situation is named in a way that intensifies the desire for change. Because these first two moments are contraries, they are mutually defined in the characterization of the world as it is and as it should be.
3. *Guilt or Responsibility.* Most commonly, this moment is an analysis of what we might call "cause" of the disruption of order. Causes may be elaborated with great complexity, or the strategy may designate a guilty individual, or fix a more focused responsibility. This aspect of interpretation of the situation constructs a narrative that narrows the focus of attention and targets change.
4. *Purification or Action.* The fourth moment names the action to be taken. Calling the action a "purification" emphasizes the dimension of appropriateness in the choice: the action must redress the guilt, remove the cause, or target the responsible.
5. *Redemption.* In this fifth moment, Burke emphasizes the nature of the scheme as a route to motivational catharsis. Burke's construct emphasizes the psychological satisfaction of well-motivated change. Change satisfies when rhetoric provides a vision of the order restored.

Laid out in this fashion, the five moments appear to be stages or steps toward change. Logically they are, but linguistically they are not. Linguistically the choices of vocabulary and rhetorical strategy draw the five moments together into a single rhetorical complex. When George W. Bush depicts a world at peace on a bright sunny September morning, he is characterizing order, but his listeners know immediately that his narrative of the World Trade Center attacks will acquire its character in the violation of that peace. We know the contrast of the motives of the attackers with the "innocent" victims will fix responsibility and point to a war on terrorism. Thus, the naming of order and disorder is born in the vision of purification and redemption, or as Burke says: "In the business of means-selecting, instead of choosing the means with respect to the nature of the problem to be solved, one tends to *state the problem in such a way that his particular aptitude becomes the 'solution' for it*."[19] Burke views the dramatistic process with its linguistic cycle of terms as so essential to rhetorical motivation for change that he calls it "the iron law of history."[20]

The language strategies through which the various political positions define a situation are transformed into a dimension of motivation through this structure. Each of the political positions in drawing on its ideology to interpret the situation also draws upon that ideology to capture an attitude toward change in the interpretation. The degree of change supported by the ideology is marked by the relationship between the way the rhetorical strategies construct the sense of order violated and the redemption which marks the catharsis. One of the fruitful ways to see this difference is from the perspective of what Burke has labeled *the scope and circumference* of change.[21]

The *reactionary* who emphasizes purpose or principle strives for change that draws the redemptive catharsis and the original sense of order together most closely. That is, reactionaries reach catharsis when change is reduced to restoration of the universal principle that they see as violated in the situation. From the reactionary's perspective, order is a principle, disorder is its violation, and change is a restoration.

The *conservative* who emphasizes agent isolates responsibility for the disorder to individuals. Conservatives see disorder as the work of individuals who have violated individually defined responsibilities and thus acquired guilt. Among societies' institutions, the criminal justice system most closely aligns with conservative notions of disorder. The system isolates violators, affixes their responsibility through formal procedures, and provides legitimate punishment for their acts. The conservative impulse is evident in ethical and even legal scandal. The impulse we often call "containing the damage" is an effort to identify one offender who can be loaded with responsibility for the violation, thus protecting a broader circle of responsibility. This process was demonstrated most dramatically in the Watergate scandal where first the burglars, then John Mitchell, then John Dean, then John Erlichman and Bob Haldeman were fixed with responsibility to save Richard Nixon. The policy failed in Watergate, but it succeeded more fully as Oliver North became the fall guy for the Iran-Contra scandal during the Reagan presidency.[22] In policy, conservatives are most likely to see problems as the result of rogue actions by individuals and propose laws to resolve the problem by punishing those rogue actions. Success in this strategy leaves the institutions of the society intact. Thus, conservative change often results in policy change, but the change is in tightening legal responsibility rather than altering institutions.

Liberals, by accepting the drift of change as natural and orderly, articulate responsibility most often in the failure to acknowledge the change of circumstances. Thus, the language of liberals describes the scene as infected with the incongruity that has grown between current circumstances and orderly change. Liberals therefore see the need to make changes in policy to realign the institutions with circumstances. The changes called for by liberals are thus more broadly focused than those sought by the conservative. The policies may find fault with and propose evolving the institutions of society.

Radicals support the broadest change of the political positions. Radicals draw the circle of responsibility around the fundamental structures of society rather than within those structures. Thus, the radical accepts the drift of change as a natural path and rejects the structure of the current system. Catharsis comes to the radical only with the dramatic change that realigns the most basic systemic character of the society.

The differences in motivation are most dramatically illustrated by comparing the positions in a single moment. The response to the terrorist attacks of September, 11, 2001, will do for such a comparison. Jerry Falwell and Pat Robertson expressed the opinion on Robertson's *700 Club* television program that the attacks were loosed when a vengeful God removed his protection over America because of the violations of his universal principles of right and wrong. Falwell named the offenders who had challenged God, including gays and liberals.[23] Only the culture's return to a more righteous following of those truths would restore that protection. The background against which the events played out for Falwell and Robertson was the universal principles of their Christian truths. As time has passed since the attacks, George W. Bush has increasingly emphasized a strategy that defines the violation of 9/11 as an attack on freedom. "Freedom is the Almighty's gift to every man and woman in this world," Bush has offered as a statement of the universal principle violated by the act.[24] Redemption will come only when America uses its power to redeem that principle in the world.

Bush's initial response to the events of 9/11 "to hunt down and to find those folks who committed this act"[25] was a conservative response to the events. The conservative strategy named the attackers, established those who supported them as enemies, and invited others to join the United States in redeeming the deaths by capturing or killing the guilty. In fact, as Bush has moved toward a more reactionary position on 9/11, he has strategically moved himself away from an emphasis on punishing Osama bin Laden as the perpetrator of the crimes.

Liberals were the least articulate in their responses to 9/11. So dramatic were the events that they hardly seemed an appropriate fit into the drift of history. Liberal strategies emerged only as the Bush policy took shape and in response to that policy. Liberals objected to the curtailing of individual rights in the name of security. Liberal responses to 9/11 placed emphasis on gathering intelligence that would provide a grasp of the situation on the ground and on the use of internationally sanctioned action, a nod to the drift toward international structures of control. John Kerry's proposal in the first presidential debate of 2004 is typical: "I have a better plan to be able to fight the war on terror by strengthening our military, strengthening our intelligence, by going after the financing more authoritatively, by doing what we need to do to rebuild the alliances, by reaching out to the Muslim world."[26] Although the roots of liberal ideology are perceivable in these strategies, the statement lacks the depth of connection to ideology. Any sense of liberal catharsis on terror is missing from public dialogue, even years after 9/11.

Radicals responded immediately to the attacks with questions about the motivations of the perpetrators and pointing to the exploitive relationship between the capitalist countries and the third world, including the Muslim world. Shortly after the events of 9/11, Susan Sontag wrote a critique that drew attention to the attackers' position. Sontag asked why they hated us so much, pointed to specific policies of the United States as the reason, and offered change in the policies as a redemptive response. Her position called for a fundamental reordering of the international relationship between rich and poor nations, the most dramatic changes proposed in response to 9/11.[27]

We have now explored the rhetorical strategies which characterize the unique character of each of the political positions. Those characteristics are summarized in table 4.1. Reactionaries describe events of the world in terms of their relationship to basic, unchanging, universal principles that define human purpose. Their ideological base consists in the apprehension of these principles. Reactionaries portray the events against the background of disorder caused by the drift away from these universal principles. They call for a reversal of this drift and motivate the call through their ideological faith in the principles.

Conservatives describe the events of the world in terms of the power of individuals to choose and the corrupting disorder of the wrong choice. Events are narrated as the actions of individuals who assume responsibility for the disorder created by their actions. Conservatives urge the isolation and purging of the offending individuals through the established institutions of social correction as the surest method of reaffirming morality and legal order.

Table 4.1.   Rhetorical Strategies of the Four Political Positions

Political Position	Description Originates in:	Breadth of Change	Catharsis in:
Reactionary	Purpose or principle	Reaffirmation of principle	Restoration of principle
Conservative	Agent	Individuals	Locating and punishing those responsible
Liberal	Scene	Accommodation to the drift	Aligning scene with drift
Radical	Agency	Structure of institutions	Adopting a structure required by drift

Liberals describe the events of the world in terms of a movement against a background of an evolving drift of change. The give and take of the process of adaptation to these changes energizes the narrative of the events. The drift of change becomes the scene of struggle to design and fine tune institutions to govern the evolving world. Liberals view people as contributing the most to peace and order when they are allowed to exercise free choice within the process of adaptation. Liberals motivate policy through descriptions of the changing scene for human endeavor and the need for adaptation to that evolution.

Radicals describe the events of the world in terms of the growing illegitimacy of current structures moving too slowly to respond to the drift of society. Radicals portray events as evidence of the growing failure of current institutions to address events. The changes they propose are the most dramatic of the four political positions and are motivated by a vision of institutions more appropriate to the changed world.

We pointed in chapter 3 to the long tradition of political positions as a meaningful stimulus to the healthy debate at the core of American democracy. We believe that the political positions can once again serve as important tools, as they have for over two centuries, if a reliable way of identifying their pragmatic characteristics once again emerges. The clustering of leaders and citizens around the symbolic identification provided by the positions promises to produce vitality and debate, strengthening the fabric of engagement necessary to full democracy.

FOUR PARABLES FROM THE POLITICAL POSITIONS

Robert Reich in *Tales of a New America: The Anxious Liberal's Guide to the Future* describes four parables that have continually surfaced as enduring ways of telling the stories of American history. These parables are rhetorical figures drawn upon as frameworks for interpreting the American experience. Some of the tales are conservative while others are liberal, but the four tales are additional rhetorical figures to be drawn upon by the four political positions in connecting to their ideology. In fact, these tales have endured because the use of each frames political issues from the characteristics of the political positions.

Reich explains that each American is familiar with some variation of what is essentially a morality tale. One such tale describes some young child who stood up against the class bully when he was picking on a small classmate. Then, in high school, the teen was very busy in sports and other school activities, excelling in all of them. As an adult, he or she served with honor in the military or went into law, education, or industry and immediately advanced beyond all expectations. Such stories are essentially myths that define Americans' national self-image. Reich states, "The American morality tale defines our understanding of who we are, and of what we want for ourselves and one another."[28]

Reich's parables are the Mob at the Gates, the Triumphant Individual, the Benevolent Community, and the Rot at the Top. The Mob at the Gates uses the language of reactionaries. Reich indicates that it is a story "about tyranny and barbarism that lurks 'out there.' " Mystically, America is "a small island of freedom and democracy in a perilous sea."[29] The tale serves as a reason for America to isolate itself against the outsiders who could overwhelm the nation. America is a beacon of the light of virtue in a world of darkness. The mystical and polemic contest of good and evil in the tale corresponds very well to the reactionary ideology. For example, the Mob at the Gate metaphor captures the reactionaries' concern that allowing in too many immigrants will threaten the way of life and standard of living in the United States.

The Triumphant Individual is a story about "The little guy who works hard, takes risks, believes in himself, and eventually earns wealth, fame, and honor." The story is about "the self-made man, or, more recently, woman who bucks the odds, spurs the naysayers, and shows what can be done with enough drive and guts."[30] The Triumphant Individual parable as a morality story focuses on the individual, and focus on the individual or agent reflects the conservative position.

The Benevolent Community is a liberal parable, a "story of neighbor and friends rolling up their sleeves and pitching in to help one another, of self-sacrifice, community pride and patriotism"[31] The story champions positive government programs in the name of the people, such as Franklin D. Roosevelt's "New Deal" and Harry Truman's "Fair Deal." As we know, liberals view public action against the background of the immediate scene or setting.

The quality of individual actions in this story comes from the quality of the benevolent community within which public actions are set.

The parable of the Rot at the Top expresses radical ideology. This story "is about the malevolence of powerful elites, be they wealthy aristocrats, capricious business leaders, or imperious government officials."[32] It is a story of powerful forces at the levers of control grinding away at those without power. In both its vision of an ideal order of equality and its focus on the power of the system, the parable suggests the egalitarian view of the radical. Since the parable promotes equality and rejects hierarchy, it frames events in the radical ideology.

The fact that Reich presents these as enduring stories that correspond with the strategies of the political positions suggests that these positions have been strong in American society over an extended period of time. They serve as enduring frameworks in which specific facts can be presented to make sense of the world. The parables function as rhetorical figures for each of the political positions, capturing their values and promising the catharsis of their motivational ideology.

THE DYNAMISM OF SPEAKERS FOR THE POLITICAL POSITIONS

In the preceding pages, we have differentiated the political positions and their characteristic strategies, illustrating them with speeches and articles framed in the appropriate strategies. We have also illustrated the differences in the varying interpretations of a single moment that shape debate about the appropriate public response to that moment. The politics of personality so prevalent in the early twenty-first century stimulates an urge to use the system to identify the political positions of particular speakers. Indeed, we also use the system for such purposes. But alas, the dynamism of individual speakers requires a sensitive reading of their oeuvre. Senator John McCain of Arizona, for example, is generally identified as a conservative and most often chooses the rhetorical strategies we have identified with conservatives. But on selected issues, McCain reasons from external facts and truths and promotes political change in strategies we identify with the liberal political position. Our experience in reading many leaders with the system is that each develops a general tendency of the ideology and political positions to which he or she turns to interpret and react to the world. But there is variation around that central tendency on particular issues or in particular situations.

Often the variation is strategic. For example, we have noted the tendency of election campaigns to move candidates toward the political middle as the season passes from the primaries into the general election. George W. Bush illustrates how a person can move back and forth between conservative, re-actionary, and liberal in a campaign. He started campaigning in the 2000 pres-idential primaries with the slogan "Compassionate Conservative." The term "compassionate" implied liberal, and when it was tied to conservative, it sug-gested Bush was near the political middle. He then moved to the right as he spoke at Bob Jones University attacking Senator John McCain. There he ap-pealed to the hard-core conservatives who were the power base of the Re-publican Party. With the nomination in hand, he moved back toward the mid-dle. By the Republican Convention, he was focusing on a role for the federal government in shaping education, a traditionally local responsibility, by stressing the effect of the quality of education on the future of students throughout their life.[33] This location of political motivation in *scene* is liberal in rhetorical form. However, we have documented how, since 9/11, Bush has moved his foreign policy toward argument from purpose.

In fact, Bush's movement from conservative to reactionary after 9/11 is ev-ident on other issues and in his speaking generally. Bush's 2004 State of the Union Address illustrates the depth of this movement. Bush opened the ad-dress by personifying America, calling the country to its responsibilities or purpose: "America this evening is a Nation called to great responsibilities. And we are rising to meet them." He next delivered a tribute to "American servicemen and women . . . bringing hope to the oppressed, and delivering justice to the violent . . . making America more secure." Beginning with per-sonification and an encomium to soldiers seems a conservative strategy be-cause it explains the moment in terms of the people who drive it. But in both cases, in Bush's view, these agents obtained their character from their com-mitments to purpose. As the speech proceeded, purpose became the central motivational force. Bush turned to deductive argument from principle as a central argumentative strategy. In the close, the purpose was bathed in the mystical light of a religious calling:

> The cause we serve is right, because it is the cause of all mankind. The mo-mentum of freedom in our world is unmistakable—and it is not carried forward by our power alone. We can trust in that greater power that guides the unfolding of the years. And in all that is to come, we can know that His purposes are just and true.[34]

Political action in the motivational rhetoric of this speech began as the prod-uct of well-made human choices, but it became a pursuit of central American purposes and principles, even to the extreme of aligning those purposes with deity. In Bush's language choices, the cause is what associates with right, and what is right is sanctioned by a higher purpose. The higher purpose functions to unfold the present and guide the future.

One other point about the dynamism of political positions is worth adding: in presidential politics the political extremes—reactionary and radical—are not generally represented because an electable candidate needs a broad base of support. In fact, most candidates who move away from the middle during the primary campaign move back toward the center for the general election. The exception to this general rule is when the country is politically polarized. In that case, a person who is close to being reactionary or radical may still have widespread support. Polarization may force candidates away from the center in search for winning coalitions. Thus, the political divisions of the early twenty-first century may create a time when reactionary rhetoric is more acceptable in mainstream political discourse.

Much of the confusion that we find in politics early in the twenty-first century is the juxtaposition of a politics of personality with strategies that exacerbate the movement of our leaders from one political position to another. Leaders who are more weakly connected to a consistent ideology become a more difficult symbol of ideology. Thus, a politics of personality becomes a politics without grounding in ideology, and the problems we described in chapter 1 emerge.

We have moved from examining each political position to begin to consider how the political positions interact to perform the coalition building that is a characteristic of well-functioning democracies. Indeed, the internal dynamics and strategies generated within each political position encourage connections between them that facilitate the work of democracy.

RHETORICAL STRATEGIES SHARED BY POLITICAL POSITIONS

In the last section, we examined specific methods to understand the rhetorical strategies chosen by the four positions. There are other strategic choices common to those of a similar political persuasion, and we should expect to find that certain strategies will emerge that unite associated political positions. We would expect to find strategies that unite the political left and political right, and others that unite the political center and political extremes. Indeed, such strategies are a feature of political discourse.

The political left—liberal and radical—and the political right—conservative and reactionary—contrast dramatically in how they approach their worlds. Burke's concept of *orientation* is useful in understanding this dichotomy. He indicates that orientation "is a bundle of judgments as to how things were, how they are, and how they may be."[35] Individual political judgments about the past, present, and future generate from an orientation. An orientation is an ideology or worldview that is brought to concrete action through embodied language choices and rhetorical strategies. For developing their values, selecting their policies, and structuring their discourse, the general orientation of the political left is external, while the right is internal. Initially, the contrast can be seen in how each approaches or defines the concept "fact" or "truth." To the political left, a fact is something in the world around us that is observable and describable, confirmable by gaining agreement among observers. To the political right, a fact is something in traditions or belief systems apprehended to be true.

External, Inductive Orientation of the Left

We pointed out in chapter 3 that the political left accepts the drift of historical change in the culture and supports changes in policy that address that drift. Because of the evolutionary nature of this characteristic, the left is sensitive to the changes that mark the evolution of society. As a result, the political left relates to the external, factual world of their experience and attributes to that factual world much more significance in selecting political action. Essentially, the left reduces questions of policy to questions of fact, which explains why liberals and radicals rely heavily on facts and statistics in their discourse. Senator Dianne Feinstein illustrated this as she looked to external facts and statistics to argue that the United States has a duty to act to reduce the greenhouse effect: "With only four percent of the world's population, we produce 20 percent of the world's greenhouse gas emissions."[36]

True to this external orientation, the political left tends to reason and structure its discourse inductively. The left examines and describes the conditions in the world and then step-by-step moves to appropriate action. For example, Senator John McCain revealed a liberal position as he debated the Climate Stewardship Act. McCain, a Republican, is known as a conservative, not a liberal, but he often takes the liberal position on particular issues. McCain started with a visual strategy that presented the scene as a series of pictures of Mt. Kilimanjaro losing snow because of global warming. He described three conclusions regarding the problem:

> Number one, greenhouse gases are increasing in the atmosphere because of human activities and they are trapping increasingly more heat. Number two, increased amounts of greenhouse gases are projected to cause irreparable harm as they lead to increased global temperatures and higher sea levels. Number three, the gases we emit to the atmosphere today will remain for decades longer.

McCain listed the ten states willing to "join New York in developing a regional strategy in the Northeast to reduce greenhouse gas emissions." McCain revealed an orientation in the indisputable scientific facts. His two pictures, one from 1993 and the other from 2000, documented externally that the snows of Kilimanjaro may soon disappear. He then stated, "These are the facts. These are facts that cannot be refuted by any scientist or any union or any special interest."[37] He reasoned from these facts to the need for action. Journalist Mark Hertsgaard demonstrated an external orientation in taking a radical position: "The environment, however, has been one bad story after another. Every week seems to bring news of a fresh abomination, from making environmental assessments in the national forests optional, to excusing the country's dirtiest power plants from upgrading the pollution controls, to stripping protection from 20 million acres of wetlands, to recycling nuclear waste within consumer goods."[38] Hertsgaard's language is abstract, but oriented toward the external world of experience.

The political left formulates inductive arguments rooted in empirical circumstances to motivate political action. To the left, these circumstantial arguments capture the evolution of society. They embrace change. They reason from these circumstances in seeking solutions to the problem. They may differ in the extent to which structure must be changed to address the problem, but their common argumentative strategy often pairs them in pursuit of change.

Internal, Deductive Orientation of the Right

In chapter 3, we noted that the political right resists the drift of society. They do so because they believe that effective policy is grounded in unchanging principles and social practices rather than in changing circumstances. The political right starts with the traditional cultural values learned through history or apprehended as foundational. The right uses the internalized values as philosophical standards for assessing experience in the external world. Any behavior or policy that conforms to their traditional values is good, and what does not is bad. Essentially, the right reduces issues and questions of policy to questions of value. This language was acted out in the 2004 presidential campaign as George W. Bush reduced the "war on terror" to a battle between "good and evil" in which other countries were either "for us or against us."

In his article "Oh, No! That '70s Show," Jerry Taylor of the Cato Institute illustrated the typical reactionary rhetoric. The article opened with a rhetorical figure that associated the current energy proposals with the trite cultural symbols of a bygone 1970s: bell bottoms, disco, and the television program *Happy Days*. Taylor portrayed the energy proposal as a reiteration of Jimmy Carter's search for control of energy use in that long ago decade. Taylor then contrasted this frivolous interventionist approach with the natural, curative principles of the market: "Washington has always been convinced that energy is somehow different from other commodities, different enough that it can't be left to the market." Taylor argued throughout the article that having violated the principle of the market, we will suffer the consequences in the form of higher prices and shortages. The article closed with a reaffirmation of the natural power of the principle: "Energy markets are important, but that's no reason for government to mess with them."[39] Taylor's article elevated the principle of the natural functioning market as a way to rationalize purpose, thus generating his motivation for policy to restore that principle.

The right, in contrast to the left, thinks and speaks deductively. A deductive approach considers a resolution or principle first before determining how the data and circumstances of the world conform to it. Richard Weaver called this approach argument by genus or definition. Weaver argued that this was the most ethical form of reasoning about public matters. In doing so, Weaver revealed his conservative roots.[40] Spokespersons usually start by stating the values and principles related to an issue and then apply them as standards to evaluate and act in a world that they usually believe is deteriorating or even falling apart. In the 2004 presidential campaign, Bush usually initiated his discussion of the hostilities in Iraq with a statement of resolve and his goal of spreading "freedom" to the people in the Middle East.

Senator Chuck Hagel's speech on the Climate Stewardship Act reasoned deductively, from the spirit of goodwill and environmental commitment that he believed human nature provided. Thus, his commitment to deductive, internal reasoning was based in the conservative tradition, faith in individual decision making. Early in his speech, Hagel transformed the issue into one of goodwill: "There is no Member of Congress who wants dirty air, dirty water, a dirty environment, or declining standards of living for their children and grandchildren." Reasoning from this basic agreement on the commitment to the environment, Hagel opposed the mandatory controls of the act and favored instead voluntary control and partnerships with developing nations to solve environmental problems. Hagel closed with a final appeal to "gradual effective change" that "is least painful to individuals, industries and nations."[41]

Complexity and the Political Middle

Another way that the political positions cluster is in strategies that separate the political middle from the political extremes. In addition to their differences over acceptance of the current institutional structure, discussed in chapter 3, the middle positions—conservative and liberal—view the world as more complex and less a unity, while the extremes—reactionary and radical—treat the world as less complex and more a unity. As a result, the political middle approaches problems more incrementally, fine tuning the structure. The political extremes view the needed change as much more dramatic, overturning the structure.

Those in the political middle view the world as complex. They believe that human experience contains a complex mix of interacting problems and issues. In the face of such complexity, actions may be narrowly targeted. Problems are viewed as sufficiently independent so that problem solving or policy may treat the issues separately and thus treat the structure incrementally. For example, conservatives and liberals generally portray the problems of inflation, capitalism, and unemployment as separately treatable. Because issues and problems necessarily interact, they are aware of, and must take into consideration, the interrelationships or multicausations linking the various problems. Such linkages imply that all actions and their effects are tentative, to be revised when human choice (conservatives) or changing circumstances (liberals) demand. The result of viewing issues as complex and problems as separated is that the political middle is unlikely to believe in conspiracies that require a coordinated, unified action. They believe the world is just too complex to control the variables required to execute a conspiracy in most areas of public policy.

The political middle's approach is illustrated by Senator John McCain's liberal speech during Senate debate on the Climate Stewardship Act, in which he enumerated three aspects of greenhouse gases and their environmental consequences, as we described earlier. McCain sees greenhouse gases as a problem that can be dealt with alone even though it is related to other environmental issues—the world is complex but treatable incrementally.

Despite the tendency to see complexity in problems, change is often easiest to accomplish when the political middle governs. There are several reasons for this. First, their acceptance of the structure and commitment to fine tuning that structure leave a smaller difference to negotiate. Once the difference is negotiated, it is easier for both to rationalize the change in terms of their ideology. The result of compromise can be accepted by the liberal as an achievement of incremental drift and by the conservative as a containment of more radical demands for change. Second, their agreement on the complexity of society permits the admission of a less than complete solution with each policy adopted. They share a view of multiple causality, which leaves a solution that both acknowledge may need to be revisited. Finally, their faith in the separability of problems means that solutions can be formulated in the areas of agreement, leaving additional approaches for different agreements.

Unity and the Political Extremes

The political extremes—reactionaries and radicals—identify a single factor that controls a number of related problems and issues. This viewpoint leaves extremists accepting the need for more radical solutions that eliminate the offending structure and replace it with a solution founded in the unity of their analysis. Such issues as inflation, insufficient capitalization, and unemployment are generally grouped and treated under the issue of the economic system—the reactionary defending the classical market, the radical rejecting capitalist exploitation. As a result, reactionaries and radicals usually see a common cause or a single causation within problems. Their acceptance of single causation makes them more likely to accept conspiracies as an explanation for events. Each extreme position has a single story that accounts for most of the problems in the world. Traditionally, the communist conspiracy was the story the extreme right used to describe the enemy. With the fall of the Soviet Union, communism lost its power. Today, "terrorism" is emerging as the enemy of the right. For the extreme left, their story traditionally has been the abuses of the capitalist system.

Mark Hertsgaard's article "A New Ice Age?" illustrates the radical extremists' tendency to use a narrower story line to explain broader issues. He opened by predicting environmental disasters such as mega-droughts, mass starvation, and nuclear exchange in the near future and traces this to the impact of global warming. He viewed the needs in environmental policy as totalized: to abandon today's dead-end approach. His structural solution was to have the World Bank "halt all coal loans immediately and all oil loans by 2108" and "increase renewable energy loans 20% per year." He then argued that these changes would be a revolutionary change. He called for "A policy to restore our damaged ecosystems and transform our technologies toward renewable energy and environmental sustainability."[42]

IDEOLOGICAL GROUNDS FOR POLITICAL ALLIANCES

James Madison called democracy an art of constructing coalitions. The similarities between adjoining political positions facilitates coalition building. Positions on the political left and the political right can develop an influence on each other. In the 2004 political campaign, the vacillation within the Democratic Party between radicals and liberals was evident in the discourse of the Democratic Convention. Though on different issues and between conservative and reactionaries, the same vacillation marked speeches of dispute and unity within the Republican Convention. We have remarked on the relative ease of compromise and successful change when conservative George W. Bush and liberal Edward M. Kennedy agree on educational reform.

Forming coalitions at greater distance along the political spectrum is much more difficult. Control of governmental policy by the extremes is inherently paradoxical because then they would no longer be the extremes. Such efforts lead to unproductive polemics and little change in adopted policy. Perhaps the affinity of the extreme right for authoritarian governments and of the extreme left for revolution returns to the hostility toward coalition between their extreme positions.

CONCLUSION

We began this project with a description of the practice of political communication in the United States early in the twenty-first century. We traced many of the dysfunctional characteristics of modern governance to the style of that communication. We particularly focused on the tendency of the science of political communication to separate political action from its ideological underpinnings. We next made the case for the importance of ideology in democracy, particularly American democracy. Ideology, we argued, is more than a mere label useful as a stimulation to achieve citizen response. In a well-functioning democracy, ideology provides the deeper sense of orientation around which political coalition forms and from which a consistency of political action is built. We called for a revitalized political communication in which political motives are well grounded in ideology.

Chapters 3 and 4 have developed a system for understanding political positions as an illustration of how rhetorical strategies can reconnect political action to ideology. The four political positions—radical, liberal, conservative, and reactionary—not only generate different approaches to political issues but also enact different strategies to motivate those strategies in ideology. The concepts we have developed in these pages form a coherent system for analyzing political discourse to revitalize the political positions as useful symbols of political motivation. Our presentation of the system began in chapter 3 with the substitution of functional definitions of the positions for traditional definitions tied to ephemeral policy stands. Those definitions grew from the characteristic attitude of each political position toward change. In this chapter, we have analyzed the rhetorical strategies through which the selection and assembly of the specifics of political discourse—facts cited, values invoked, causes attributed, policies proposed—are woven together into messages that motivate public action within the consistency of political philosophy or ideology.

These strategies provide depth to political communication. They connect the ephemeral interpretation of a political moment into more consistent attitudes about change and the role of government in change. Finally, the system also explored the possibilities for relationships among the strategies characteristic of the four political positions. Because the political positions share attitudes toward the viability of the current social structure or toward the drift of current policy, natural points of barrier and possibility for coalition emerge across the political spectrum. Thus the motivation for coalition, so vital to a properly functioning democracy, can emerge from the strategic opportunities opened in the relationships among political positions.

As a system for rhetorical analysis, the work of chapters 3 and 4 opens a view on current political communication and suggests new emphases that would enhance democratic practice. In using the system over a number of years, we have found it particularly useful in organizing debate on particular issues. The functional definitions suggest the possibilities in approaching public problems. The ability to discern differing strategies and their ideological antecedents encourages attention to a full diversity of voices addressing the problem. An understanding of the rhetorical possibilities of each political position should suggest new directions for developing legitimate democratic response.

More to the point of our current political moment—the confused gridlock of early twenty-first-century politics—we believe that revitalizing terminologies such as the four political positions provides a vocabulary that facilitates the enrichment of political motivation that we find lacking. If political positions are to serve as symbolic touchstones through which political debate can organize, and around which coalitions of support can form, their role in political communication must be discernible. Revitalizing the political positions as symbolic touchstones does the rhetorical work of "ideographs" that we talked about in chapter 2: "Ideographs," Michael Calvin McGee writes, "are one-term sums of an orientation. . . . The important fact about ideographs is that they exist in real discourse, functioning clearly and evidently as agents of political consciousness."[43] The terminology of the political positions has this capacity to place policy into ideological orientation in a way that clearly and evidently organizes the democratic public into an effective decision-making process.

In this chapter, we have drawn upon several examples of what Kenneth Burke would call "rounded statements about motive" to illustrate the rhetorical strategies that differentiate the four political positions and the orientations of the left, right, middle, and extremes. Although such well-rounded statements were available to us, we find them all too rarely in modern political discourse. We would urge that political leaders and citizens strive to achieve such fullness. When we focus on these statements, several characteristics they share come to our attention. First, they are *well-rounded*, that is, they provide a complete and coherent account of their moment, a comprehensive understanding. The excessive reduction of so much modern political communication seeks response without such completeness of understanding. Second, they provide *depth of understanding*. They give reasons for actions they would propose.

This connects them with the events of the world, with the values of the culture, with the cooperation of other citizens. All of the virtues of ideology in a well-functioning democracy come to the fore with this achievement of depth. Third, they *tie actions to basic beliefs* about how political action is properly chosen. In other words, they provide the basis for legitimacy. Ideology contains these judgments of appropriateness, and the connection with ideology brings them into play. Fourth, these statements *provide bases for agreement and cooperation* among leaders and citizens seeking to use political means to better their society. Fifth, these statements offer *catharsis* in addressing events in day-to-day life. They define success. They delineate processes. In this way, they provide the sense of social accomplishment so nurturing to democracy. Finally, when such statements are frequent enough, they provide a *consistency* in the political landscape that fosters identification of leaders and citizens in pursuit of common goals and in addressing commonly felt problems. They form a denser fabric of democratic experience.

Political positions are useful symbols of the coalition building that James Madison pointed to as the secret of America's style of democracy. If political discourse again achieves a consistency that permits leaders and citizens to cluster around political positions, the positions can once again take their place as central symbols in the rich texture of debate that characterizes American democracy.

NOTES

1. The intellectual movement called contextualism is most clearly explained by Stephen Pepper, *World Hypotheses* (Berkeley: University of California Press, 1942), 232–79. In the study of communication, the movement is explained by James E. Ford and James F. Klumpp, "Systematic Pluralism: An Inquiry into the Bases of Communication Research," *Critical Studies in Mass Communication* 2 (1985): 408–29. For more discussion of Pepper's world hypotheses and root metaphors, see Mark E. Huglen and Basil B. Clark, *Poetic Healing: A Vietnam Veteran's Journey from a Communication Perspective*, revised and expanded ed. (West Lafayette, Ind.: Parlor Press, 2005), 113–15.

2. Kenneth Burke, *Permanence and Change: An Anatomy of Purpose*, 3rd ed. (1935; Berkeley: University of California Press, 1984), 31–36; 220–21.

3. Kenneth Burke, *Philosophy of Literary Form*, 3rd ed. (1941; Berkeley: University of California Press, 1973), 1.

4. Kenneth Burke, *A Rhetoric of Motives* (1950; Berkeley: University of California Press, 1969), 21.

5. Burke, *Permanence and Change*, 35.

6. Burke, *A Rhetoric of Motives*, 88.

7. Burke, *Permanence and Change*, 220.

8. Kenneth Burke, *A Grammar of Motives* (1945; Berkeley: University of California Press, 1969), 21–38.

9. Burke, *A Grammar of Motives*, xv. Italics added.

10. Burke, *Philosophy of Literary Form*, 105–6.

11. Burke, *A Grammar of Motives*, 128.

12. Burke, *A Grammar of Motives*, 15.

13. The White House, "President Addresses the Nation in Prime Time Press Conference" (April 13, 2004), www.whitehouse.gov/news/releases/2004/04/20040413-20 .html (September 24, 2004).

14. Robert Bork, *Slouching toward Gomorrah*, 2nd ed. (New York: Regan Books, 1997).

15. Ronald Reagan, "State of the Union Address" (January 25, 1984), www.usa-presidents.info/union/reagan-3.html (January 8, 2005).

16. Bill Clinton, "State of the Union Address" (January 19, 1999), www.cnn.com/ ALLPOLITICS/stories/1999/01/19/sotu.transcript/ (January 8, 2005).

17. Ralph Nader, "Iraq War and Occupation," Nader/Camejo 2004, www.votenader .org/issues/index.php?cid=17 (January 8, 2005).

18. Bernard L. Brock, "Political Speaking: A Burkean Approach," in *Critical Responses to Kenneth Burke*, ed. William H. Rueckert (Minneapolis: University of Minnesota Press, 1966), 444.

19. Burke, *Permanence and Change*, 242–43. Emphasis in original.

20. Kenneth Burke, *The Rhetoric of Religion: Studies in Logology* (Boston: Beacon Press, 1961), 4–5, 183–96.

21. Burke, *A Grammar of Motives*, 77–85.

22. For an extended example of this process at work in discourse, see James F. Klumpp and Thomas A. Hollihan, "Debunking the Resignation of Earl Butz: Sacrificing an Official Racist," *Quarterly Journal of Speech* 65 (1979): 1–11.

23. Jerry Falwell and Pat Robertson, Partial Transcript of Comments from *700 Club*, Beliefnet.com (September 13, 2001), www.beliefnet.com/story/87/story_8770_1.html (January 3, 2005).

24. George W. Bush, Press Conference, April 13, 2004.

25. The White House, "Remarks by the President after Two Planes Crash into World Trade Center" (September 11, 2001), www.whitehouse.gov/news/releases/ 2001/09/20010911.html (September 4, 2004).

26. The First Bush-Kerry Presidential Debate (September 30, 2004), www.debates .org/pages/trans2004a.html (January 3, 2005).

27. Susan Sontag, "Talk of the Town," *New Yorker*, September 24, 2001, 32.

28. Robert B. Reich, *Tales of a New America: The Anxious Liberal's Guide to the Future* (New York: Vintage Books, 1988).

29. Reich, *Tales of a New America*, 8.

30. Reich, *Tales of a New America*, 9.

31. Reich, *Tales of a New America*, 10.

32. Reich, *Tales of a New America*, 11.

33. George W. Bush, Acceptance Speech, Republican National Convention, Philadelphia (August 3, 2000), www.2000gop.com/convention/speech/speech/speech bush.html (January 9, 2005).

34. The White House, George W. Bush, State of the Union Address (January 20, 2004), www.whitehouse.gov/news/releases/2004/01/20040120-7.html (January 29, 2005).

35. Burke, *A Rhetoric of Motives*, 20.

36. Dianne Feinstein, "Should the Senate Pass S.139, the Climate Stewardship Act?" *Congressional Digest* 83, no. 1 (January 2004): 16.

37. John McCain, "Should the Senate Pass S.139, the Climate Stewardship Act?" *Congressional Digest* 83, no. 1 (January 2004): 12.

38. Mark Hertsgaard, "A New Ice Age?" *Nation*, March 1, 2004, 7–8.

39. Jerry Taylor, "Oh, No! That '70s Show: Against Carterism in Energy Policy," *National Review*, March 25, 2002, 42, 43.

40. Richard M. Weaver, *Language Is Sermonic: Richard M. Weaver on the Nature of Rhetoric*, ed. Richard L. Johannesen, Rennard Strickland, and Ralph T. Eubanks (Baton Rouge: Louisiana State University Press, 1970), 211–12.

41. Chuck Hagel, "Should the Senate Pass S.139, the Climate Stewardship Act?" *Congressional Digest* 83, no. 1 (January 2004): 13.

42. Hertsgaard, "A New Ice Age?" 7–8.

43. Michael Calvin McGee, "The 'Ideograph': A Link between Rhetoric and Ideology," *Quarterly Journal of Speech* 66 (1980): 7.

5

Beyond the Political Chaos

Where Are We Going?

We began this study by describing the divided and chaotic political land-scape in the United States at the beginning of the twenty-first century. The United States finds itself without clear political direction, in the midst of a particularly polarized time. We argued that this confusion is being prolonged by a style of discourse that cuts political action off from its ideological roots and thus retards the normal process of political give and take and the result-ing emergence of democratic legitimacy. We focused on political ideology as the fabric woven from public understanding of the world, public values that shape choice, and visions the public longs to make real. We thus called for at-tention to rhetorical strategies that motivate political action by knitting it into this fabric of ideology. A careful study of political positions as a symbolic re-source for this purpose followed. We called for language strategies rather than stands on issues to organize the political landscape. Analysis of language strategies opens a vista on attitudes toward change, rhetorical strategies, po-litical frames, and public motives that tie political action to ideology. We de-fended such attention to reuniting action and ideology as critical to the func-tioning of a healthy democracy.

At times like these, times of polemic politics in which the center fails to hold and the political extremes exercise power, the attention to language strategies has another important advantage. With these strategies to help us gaze through the political fog, we can work with the current political view-points from a broader perspective. Rather than simply seeing the current chaotic political atmosphere as malignant, we can view it as a transition to a reoriented political landscape to come. Because the language strategies are not tied to the issues of the current miasma, we can discern the emergence of new issues around which the next political configuration will turn. With the methods we have developed in this study, we now project today's politics into the future to see how political discourse is most likely to evolve in the coming years. The seeming chaos and conflict of the present reveal the potentialities of a profound transformation in American culture and politics.

IN THE MIDST OF A PARADIGM SHIFT

The chaos we described in chapter 1 is more than the reversal of party labels. We believe it reflects a deep potentiality for a transformation in our culture as the stability of the prevailing scientific worldview gives way to a new, more complex and comprehensive way of understanding the world. The ways of thinking tied to an earlier scientific age are giving way to a new paradigm.[1]

To explore the implications of this evolution, we begin by examining the relationships between the political middle and the political extremes in uncertain times. During periods of stability and incremental change, the rhetorical strategies of the political middle dominate a well-functioning public discourse. At moments of intense polarity, however, the rhetorical strategies of the political extremes become critical. At the ends of the political spectrum, the left attempts to move the middle toward greater equality and the right urges greater social control.

The visions that frame this polarized moment are evolving in the face of a deep social transformation. We look at the drift of society over time, at structural elements that enable society to move with the drift, and at language choices invoked to define, justify, and resist this drift. We emphasize how the language emerging at the extreme ends of the political spectrum is pushing and pulling the political center into a new direction. By looking at the pushing and pulling, we are able to see tensions, extensions, and contradictions to allow us to predict the new reshaped middle.

Once again, Kenneth Burke gives us a framework for exploring major changes in the orientations that provide cohesion to how people explain and understand their world. He discusses how society has moved in evolutionary stages from an orientation of magic to religion and from religion to science. Each stage, Burke argues, grows out of the contradictions and limitations of the previous period. He predicts that science, the dominant paradigm for more than three centuries, will give way to poetic humanism, an orientation toward the world that stresses collective concerns over individual benefit, ways of knowing beyond the senses, and an expanded sense of human possibility.[2]

Transformations of this magnitude are never easy or clear-cut.[3] But they are signaled by a breakdown in established categories and ways of explaining the world. Today there is a growing sense among activists and analysts alike that we are experiencing such changes. Something very different is evolving in our political world. For some, it is a deep structural change marking the end of what is called the neo-liberal ideology that has undergirded the philosophy of government in the Western world for more than fifty years.[4] For others it is the end of the political coalitions that have governed the United States since the middle of the twentieth century.[5] The sense that we are entering a new time is widespread. Kevin Phillips, writing about the relationship between democracy and wealth over the past three centuries, has described the unsettledness that marks this current period of transition:

New centuries have often been stress points in the psychology, if not the immediate fortunes, of the world's leading economic powers. Like its predecessors, the United States found its uncertainties rising sharply as the calendar turned. . . . The hung presidential election of 2000, for its part, fed skepticism about the US electoral system. September 11 added a grave concern about the future of American domestic and international security.[6]

There is a growing consensus that the transition into the new century is more than a change of date. It marks an emergence of new sensibilities, a new consciousness and way of looking at the world. It is a time of extraordinary possibilities and enormous dangers. For some, it is the possibility of the restoration of a more moral America. For others, there are the dark portends of emerging fascism. For some, it is the possibility of a new democracy. Commenting from a liberal perspective, Paul Ray and Sherry Anderson capture the sense of transformation in their work on creative cultural change when they say simply, "A whole new culture is emerging, with a greater promise than most of us have dared to dream."[7]

The promise of a more liberal, democratic future seems utopian in a world marked with war, terrorism, and brutality. Yet we believe that historically the United States has found ways to move toward an ever more inclusive and egalitarian society.[8] The drift of the last 300 years, with all its imperfections, has been toward a deeper and more expansive understanding of democracy. In the past, when confronted with choices between protecting privilege and becoming more inclusive, Americans have consistently moved on a path toward greater equality.[9] As Martin Luther King Jr., said, "The arch of the universe is long, but it bends toward justice."

There are clear signs to indicate that a deep cultural transformation is under way today. We are moving away from the paradigm of science, toward a more inclusive sense of community. This drift is not predetermined. Nor is history necessarily a guide to a more open future, for it holds as many lessons of despair as of hope.[10] The present, however, can be understood as part of a larger pattern of transition in American life helping to define the contours of a paradigm shift toward the communitarian, humanistic principles embodied in Burke's notion of poetic humanism.

In times of uncertainty and change, Burke's insights about how language shapes reality and influences actions are especially helpful in trying to understand where we are and where we are headed. Burke gives us ways to think about the future by looking dialectically at contradictions emerging in the present from the patterns that were formed in the past. He directs our thinking to incongruities and paradoxes, stretching terms, stealing back and forth symbols, and snapping words into their opposites.

TWO VIEWS OF CHANGE

The history of the United States is marked by two related experiences of change: incremental and dramatic. Much of the time we experience incremental change. The center of American politics shares a broad consensus of values, beliefs, and policies and disagrees over the pace and extent of change, but not over its fundamental direction. In times of incremental change, the political middle is generally a stable core, bound together by a cohesive set of values. Whatever the particular disagreements on policy, this stable core represents a coherent middle with a shared set of beliefs. Historian Richard Hofstader, reflecting on the development of American political traditions observes that there has been a strong "unity of culture and political tradition, upon which American culture has stood."[11] This center, sometimes called the "American creed,"[12] rests on a particular interpretation of the American experiment. During periods dominated by incremental change, the radical left and reactionary right represent smaller minorities. They are often isolated and marginal. The general drift of society is accepted, with disagreements emphasizing pace and manner of change. During the late 1950s and the presidency of Dwight Eisenhower, for example, there was broad agreement on the need to extend support for public education. While political parties of the center disagreed on the means and extent of programs, support for the goal was widespread. Likewise, the basic outline of the structures and systems that supported the drift toward greater access to education for all young people of the country was accepted by the middle.

At other moments, change has been swift and intense. In these moments of dramatic change, the more intense perspectives of the political extremes drown out the stable, cautious voices of the middle. Sometimes it is the voice of the radical left urging pragmatic change: expansion of the vote, limitation of corporate power, or creation of progressive laws to protect working people and the environment. Other times it is of the reactionary right urging the restoration of American ideals and purpose.

The radical left usually challenges the basic structures of society, arguing for significant change to accelerate the drift toward equality. Most often this radical challenge begins within the margins of social movements. The movements for women's suffrage, abolition, farmer cooperatives, labor rights, civil rights, and environmental justice are all examples of polarized moments, initiated within the extreme that then persuaded the middle to adopt significant structural change. For example, Richard Nixon as a center-right president accepted many of the Great Society programs such as Model Cities and rent subsidies initiated by his more liberal democratic predecessor, Lyndon Johnson.[13]

The extreme right, on the other hand, usually challenges the basic drift of the society and rejects the structures supporting it. It is labeled reactionary because it is reacting against the drift toward the new structure. Because the right focuses on individuals before the collectivity, the right's traditional route to creating greater equality in the world occurs through individual and privatized means (which opposes the collective and governmental means emphasized on the left). However, today the extreme right is utilizing the federal government to preserve traditional moral values and capitalist rights and power, resulting in another apparent reversal of right and left. The right highlights the need for stability and control and for the preservation of traditional values. The right and left have alternative routes to conclusions because of the strategy emphasized. The right's focus on individuals before the collective may not be the most direct route to creating equality in the world, but the left's focus on the scene and the collective before the individual may not be the most direct route to cultivating individual talent and successes.

Push and Pull between the Extremes

In our view, polarized moments emerge because of the pull toward the radical vision. That pull begins to influence the middle, provoking the reactionary right into intense entrenchment and restoration practices. From the very beginnings of the republic, the drift of the society, however imperfectly, has been compelled by the radical tradition, pushing and pulling the body politic toward a more open and generous democracy. At other periods, in reaction to this drift, the United States has been pushed toward private interests, protecting property, and establishing order. This pattern was first set in the two great founding documents: the radical Declaration of Independence with its commitment to equality as self-evident, and the Constitution with its promise of "domestic tranquility" and greater prosperity. Phillips has referred to this dynamic as the push between a radical/liberal vision of brotherhood and equality versus a reactionary/conservative vision of the accumulation of private wealth.[14] This push and pull between the political extremes and its effects on the values and policies of the political middle are the foundation of American political cycles.[15] The push and pull between the two extremes and the drift toward democracy has been described in various terms. Writing in 1841, Ralph Waldo Emerson noted, "the party of Conservatism and that of Innovation are very old . . . Innovation is the salient energy; Conservatism the pause on the last movement." Later, Henry Adams identified swings between "centralization and diffusion of national energy." In the early twentieth century, Arthur Schlesinger Sr. talked about the swings "between conservatism and liberalism, between periods of concern for the rights of the few and periods of concern for the wrongs of the many."[16]

The resolution of these polarities moves the nation as a whole forward to a new consensus on what is normal or ordinary. Each swing holds with it the newly forged agreements. Schlesinger argued that political cycles could be best understood as a "spiral" that moved the nation closer to equality with each swing, establishing the drift to the left end of the political spectrum. He observed that after each swing from the left back to the right, "liberal reforms usually survived after conservatives regained power." Thus the appropriate image "was the spiral in which alternation proceeded at successively higher levels and allowed for the accumulation of change."[17] Building on these earlier works, his son Arthur Schlesinger Jr. described cycles of American politics "as a continuing shift in national involvement, between public purpose and private interest."[18] The cycles are characterized by periods of relative stability and great polarization. In the current moment, the period of polarization is intensified by the deeper paradigm shift that undergirds the more predictable patterns of change.

Polarized Moments Give Rise to Dramatic Change

Dramatic change emerges during polarized moments. Such moments evolve as those on the radical left end of the spectrum intensify the drift toward equality by challenging existing structures. This provokes the reactions of the extreme right. Increasing polarization of the middle marks the precondition for significant cultural and political change.

Polarized moments develop as the differing visions characteristic of the extremes compete for the allegiance of those in the middle. Since the early 1960s, the United States has been in a period of deepening polarization. The deepening has an ebb and flow, but by the beginning of the new century, national opinion polls indicated that the country was divided almost in half on every major issue. Commenting on the election in 2004, Immanual Wallerstein said:

But it is clear that the electorate is both extremely polarized and almost evenly divided. The Republican Party has perhaps never been so aggressively right wing since 1936 (and they were trounced in that election). And the Democratic Party has never been so passionate in opposition to an incumbent president. The slogan, "anyone but Bush," is heard everywhere.[19]

The beginnings of this division can be found with the development of the civil rights movement. In the early 1960s, the battle over civil rights and full integration of African Americans ushered in a period of increasingly polarized political activity as people organized to create greater social and economic equality and for greater participation in the life of the nation. Radical movements such as black power, women's liberation, ecology, disarmament, alternative energy, and sustainable development all stimulated a reaction.

In discussing the implications of polarity, Kevin Phillips explained: "Levels of dissatisfaction like those seen between 1968 and 1994 rarely dissolve in anything less than a truly new economic and political era." Given the 2000 election, the 9/11 attacks, and the launching of a war on terrorism, Phillips emphasized that we face a new context in which "the shape of a new radicalism was critical."[20] Out of the contest between two competing visions—that of the radical left and that of the reactionary right—the contours of American politics shaping the future will emerge.

COMPETING VISIONS

The radical left has had a stable vision for more than 150 years, emphasizing social and economic equality. Radicals embrace the drift of society toward equality and emphasize the role of structure, or in Burke's terms "agency," in moving society more fully toward that end. Radicals, while accepting the drift, reject the existing structures or system and generate new means to advance equality. Framed by ideas of the Enlightenment that propelled the American and French Revolutions, the vision of equality has deep roots in notions of reason, limited government, and common action. For much of the past century, the dominant articulation of this vision was within the ideological framework of socialist theory. Anarchists, communists, and socialist formations represented the far left end of the spectrum. Labor unions, liberal democrats, and a host of advocacy groups associated with movements of the 1960s represented the liberal position. But with the fall of the Soviet Union in the waning days of the last century, the radical left lost focus. Still, arguing from agency, or means and structure, the radical vision of equality persists as a utopian ideal.

The Left's Vision Expands

In the late 1990s, an expanded radical vision began to develop in response to the expansion of transnational capitalism and the ideological framework of neo-liberalism. The expanded vision burst onto the public stage in the Battle of Seattle in 1999. The organized opposition to the meeting of the World Trade Organization (WTO) indicated a new group of civil actors reinvigorating the radical political scene. Drawing upon the earlier vision, the new radicals expanded to embrace principles of ecology, sustainable development, local action, spirituality, and cultural activism. Both the media and the secretary general of the United Nations have referred to them as a "new world superpower.[21]

Since the initial protest of the WTO, literally thousands of individuals and groups have traveled the globe to challenge the arrangements of international corporate capital, demanding greater transparency in decision making, in economic justice and human rights, and in sustainable development. Uniting under a banner proclaiming "another world is possible," many groups see themselves as part of a radical civil society made up of locally based organizations responding to the ravages of global capital. They have been consciously broadening their scope of action, positioning themselves as the representatives of a new global civil network in opposition to the corporate, governmental structure. Almost without notice, they have set the stage for a new form of collective action and have become a potent force in world politics, swelling in number from a few thousand organizations a decade ago to tens of thousands today (more than 20,000 of them international or transnational) and from fewer than 300 recognized by the United Nations in 1970 to close to 3,000 today. Such newly emerging formations are developing networks of political activists, grassroots groups, social movements, and coalitions in what has been dubbed "global civil society."[22] They are defining a powerful resistance movement to counter runaway globalization and neo-liberalism.

The language choices found within this newly emerging radical movement still emphasize the twin concerns of the radical political orientation. They emphasize the rejection of the current structural arrangements of society and an effort to accelerate the movement of society as a whole toward equality and justice. This consistency of language choice is evident in the work of Naomi Klein, who has helped define the new radicalism. As a radical, she decided to join the "anybody but Bush" camp and engage in an electoral campaign to emphasize the importance of thinking about structural relationships (agency) rather than personalities (agent).

It's worth remembering that it was under Bill Clinton that the progressive movements in the west began to turn our attention to systems again: corporate globalization, even—gasp—capitalism and colonialism. We began to understand modern empire not as the purview of a single nation, no matter how powerful, but a global system of interlocking states, international institutions and corporations, an understanding that allowed us to build global networks in response, from the World Social Forum to Indymedia. Innocuous leaders who spout liberal platitudes while slashing welfare and privatizing the planet push us to better identify those systems and to build movements agile and intelligent enough to confront them.[23]

The Right's Vision Responds

The reactionary right, too, has had a stable vision of the future for more than 150 years. Since the earliest days of abolition and the rising industrial economy of the North, the reactionary right has advocated a unified perspective rooted in its view of God's purpose for America and an interpretation of the natural order of the world. Arguing from purpose and principle, the reactionary extreme holds as its view that God has ordained America to fulfill the "best hope of man." In this view, the United States has a divine mission that can only be accomplished when those ordained by God to be in charge rule. Generally, this vision places a man at the head of the family and the nation. In the well-ordered universe, these ordained rulers have a duty to make decisions, accumulate resources, and have dominion over the land. The effort to fulfill this destiny has been thwarted by the erosion of culture through the corrupt influence of people of color, women, liberals, gay and lesbian people, and selfish individuals. In this vision, the reactionary right longs for the restoration of a stable and controlled community, with men at the head of their households and all others in their proper place.[24] The extreme reactionary right is represented by such organizations as the Ku Klux Klan, the American Nazi Party, the John Birch Society, Skinheads, the Posse Comitatus or Militia Movement, and the Christian Identity Movement. The conservative arm of the Republican Party is usually typified by such figures as Barry Goldwater, Ronald Reagan, and George H. W. Bush. Toward the middle of the spectrum are moderate Republicans like Dwight Eisenhower, Nelson Rockefeller, and Richard Nixon.

The tenacity of this vision, and a more reactionary expression, can be seen in the words of Pat Robertson and Jerry Falwell shortly after the terrorist attacks on September 11, 2001. Falwell spoke on Robertson's *700 Club* about the cause of the attacks: "What we saw on Tuesday, as terrible as it is, could be minuscule if, in fact, God continues to lift the curtain and allow the enemies of America to give us probably what we deserve." Robertson expressed his agreement. Then Falwell went on:

The ACLU has got to take a lot of blame for this. And I know I'll hear from them for this, but throwing God . . . successfully with the help of the federal court system . . . throwing God out of the public square, out of the schools, the abortionists have got to bear some burden for this because God will not be mocked and when we destroy 40 million little innocent babies, we make God mad. . . . I really believe that the pagans and the abortionists and the feminists and the gays and the lesbians who are actively trying to make that an alternative lifestyle, the ACLU, People for the American Way, all of them who try to secularize America . . . I point the thing in their face and say you helped this happen.[25]

Over the last three decades, the extreme reactionary right vision has been gaining power within the more moderate and middle of society. The election of Ronald Reagan in 1980 signaled the triumph of the right that had been struggling since 1964 to move the Republican Party away from the more center-liberal positions that had dominated the middle since the New Deal coalition of Franklin Roosevelt. For the next twenty-five years there was a strong pull toward the reactionary ends of the spectrum, emphasizing stability, Christian values, control, and the use of military power. The so-called culture wars, for example, dominated much of the political debate during this period. Prayer in school, abortion, public displays of the Ten Commandments, the role of fundamentalist Christian values in public policy, and the sense of the United States as a chosen nation were interwoven in public debates, policies, and programs.[26] In the presidential election of 2004, the reactionary Christian right was widely credited with the Bush victory as exit polls showed that values were considered more important than the war on terrorism, the war in Iraq, or the economy.[27]

For the last two decades of the twentieth century and into the beginning of the twenty-first, the extreme reactionary right has had the most influence on the conservative and middle positions. It has even pulled the liberal positions toward the right end of the political spectrum, isolating radicals. The victory of George W. Bush for a second term in 2004 demonstrated the vast electoral appeal of the right-reactionary vision of a stable, controlled, purposeful America to a narrow majority of voters.

At the same time, the traditional vision of the reactionary right has begun to reveal tensions. A new group of reactionary-conservative thinkers and organizers nurtured under the Reagan and Bush administrations began to articulate a more reactionary agenda. As the ideology within this new group began to evolve, these neo-conservatives rejected the more traditional isolationist, small government views of the political right. They demonstrated a willingness to use government to foster a fundamentalist Christian-based social agenda and to use American military power to achieve political and economic ends on a global scale. The neo-conservative vision exerted influence on the center, moving it into the general policies of the Republican Party under George W. Bush.[28]

EXTREME VISIONS ENGAGE THE MIDDLE

We have noted that the struggle between polar visions to influence the middle dominates political discourse in times of dramatic change. Even in periods of incremental change, it is the vision of the extremes that animates the ideological visions projected toward the middle. Liberals and those on the left to center are influenced by the radical ideology, and conservatives and those on the right to center are influenced by the reactionary ideology.

To project the direction of American politics we look first at the major polarities dominating the present and at how they are changing the mainstream. For as politics evolve, elements of each of the extreme visions become accepted or rejected by the broad middle. For example, the core right-wing value of individual achievement is broadly accepted by the middle, just as the core left-wing value of racial equality is now a widely held value.

Over the last few decades, four primary tension points or contested perspectives have framed the pull for stability and control and the push toward equality. They are expressed in the following polarities:

- Christian fundamentalist culture vs. pluralistic culture
- Hierarchical society vs. egalitarian society
- Controlled, obedient, populace vs. creative, critically questioning individuals
- American exceptionalism and nationalism with the unilateral use of force vs. international cooperation and negotiation with the growth of international institutions

These polarities are dialectical opposites that provide the framework for the radical and reactionary visions as they currently influence discourse by attracting and influencing the middle.

Democrats, for example, who are generally within the liberal to left end of the political continuum, tend toward a more multicultural, less hierarchical, creative worldview and prefer emphasizing cooperative international action to achieve American goals. Republicans, who are generally within the conservative to right end of the spectrum, tend toward a more Christian-centered, hierarchical, controlled worldview and believe in the use of unilateral force when necessary to achieve American goals. David Brooks captured these differing orientations in a tongue-in-cheek piece about likely campaign contributors in the 2004 presidential election: "There are two sorts of people in the information-age elite, spreadsheet people and paragraph people. Spreadsheet people work with numbers, wear loafers and support Republicans. Paragraph people work with prose, don't shine their shoes as often as they should and back Democrats."[29]

Within the framework of these dialectical opposites, the political middle attempts to carve out areas for discussion, agreement, compromise, and policies. The capacity of the political middle to hold a broadly shared consensus can be seen in the presidential campaign of 2004. George W. Bush and John Kerry reflected several major areas of agreement. While the election was characterized by negative and often bitter policy disagreements, both candidates articulated shared perspectives, indicating their understanding of the arguments most likely to influence the political middle. At the same time, they were able to distinguish themselves within each area, simultaneously creating a sense of where they were unified and where divided.

Both candidates, for example, accepted a view of the country as more culturally diverse than just two decades earlier. Bush, as a right of center Republican, portrayed an inclusive view of leadership, indicating the degree to which the drift toward multiculturalism has become a part of the general society. During his first term as president, Bush appointed African Americans, Hispanics, and women to high cabinet positions and ran a campaign that overtly projected a multicultural image. At the Republican Convention, California Governor Arnold Schwarzenegger illustrated the conservative position, emphasizing individual achievement with the general acceptance of all who share in a core set of beliefs, regardless of ethnic or cultural differences. Drawing on his own story as a poor immigrant who achieved success, he said:

> To my fellow immigrants listening tonight, I want you to know how welcome you are in this party. We Republicans admire your ambition. We encourage your dreams. We believe in your future. One thing I learned about America is that if you work hard and play by the rules, this country is truly open to you. You can achieve anything . . . in this country it doesn't make any difference where you were born. It doesn't make any difference who your parents were. . . . America gave me opportunities, and my immigrant dreams came true.[30]

While acknowledging this drift toward equality and the view of a more multicultural society, Bush extended rhetorical and strategic connections to the more reactionary extremes in his party by limiting his acceptance of multiculturalism to people of color and immigrant groups. Consistent with a conservative view, people from these groups were accepted not as representatives of a collective culture or identity, but as individuals who had triumphed over adversity to achieve success.[31] Also consistent with his conservative-reactionary stance, Bush made clear his rejection of the drift toward greater inclusion. He drew the line of inclusion at people in same-sex relationships. To underscore his rejection of the drift, Bush endorsed several statewide initiatives to ban same-sex marriage and backed an amendment to the Constitution on this issue. Bush moved farther toward the reactionary position as he rejected the existing structural mechanisms designed to encourage multiculturalism. Early in his first term, for example, Bush directed the Justice Department to abandon its historic support for Affirmative Action and to argue against race as a factor in university admissions in the University of Michigan case brought before the Supreme Court.[32]

John Kerry, as a liberal Democrat, joined Bush in his opposition to same-sex marriage, separating himself from the extreme left end of the spectrum. However, Kerry made rhetorical and strategic connections to the radical vision of inclusion. He spoke in favor of civil unions and an end to discrimination against all people. Further, Kerry differed with Bush on Affirmative Action, defending it as an important and needed structural mechanism.

On international issues, similar areas of agreement and disagreement were evident. Both Bush and Kerry agreed with the decision to invade Iraq. Kerry, the Democrat, functioning within the liberal perspective, emphasized the role of multinational action; Bush, the Republican, insisted on the right of the United States to act alone in its own interest. Kerry accepted the idea of the United Nations as an important international body; Bush, again in a bow to the reactionary viewpoint, disparaged it, defending the "doing it alone" attitude of the reactionaries.

People in the middle then move along the continuum between the opposite polls, differing on both the extent to which they support the drift of the society and the degree to which they are willing to embrace or alter structures. The lens through which people evaluate the world and respond to issues further differentiates the positions of individuals, parties, and organizations on the political continuum. For the middle-right conservative, the role of individuals, or in Burke's terms, agent, is essential. In Schwarzenegger's speech to the Republican Convention in 2004, we find a strong emphasis on the individual. The governor of California provides a succinct statement of the moderate party position:

> If you believe that government should be accountable to the people, not the people to the government . . . then you are a Republican! If you believe a person should be treated as an individual, not as a member of an interest group . . . then you are a Republican! If you believe your family knows how to spend your money better than the government does . . . then you are a Republican.[33]

For the middle-left, scenic elements or changing circumstances provide the motives for action.

THE ORIGINS OF CHANGE

Society leans toward consensus, and polarities demand resolution. Still, new circumstances emerge, requiring interpretations and responses. The issues and debates that polarize one moment in time come to resolution and flow from the extreme to the middle, forging a new public consensus on political issues that were once divisive. The changes brought by the force of circumstance and the resolution of earlier divisions force new alignments as the political middle absorbs an expanded sense of what is ordinary and normal. Thus the political positions on the continuum are never static in their political stands, but constantly evolving in a context of change. As we look into the future, we base our predictions on what we believe are the primary forces for change surging through today's political landscape.

Today, three distinct forces are evolving to reshape the political landscape, giving rise to new polarities to stretch the visions of the political extremes. On a deep, more slowly moving level, the first force is the shift in paradigm from science to poetic humanism.[34] The growing emphasis on values, personal narratives, and metaphors of human experience has marked our public discourse. The second is the cyclical pattern of American political trends. Having moved rightward for more than forty years, almost all cyclical viewpoints suggest that we are reaching a zenith in this swing to the right. History tells us that this domination by the right wing, with its emphasis on stability and the protection of private interests, is increasing pressure for a swing in the other direction toward a more left-liberal public-interest orientation.[35] These deeply felt cyclical shifts are furthered by the tensions and contradictions that necessarily emerge in the clash between an ever changing reality and stable, core concepts held by extreme visions.

Third, as deep paradigm and cyclical patterns evolve, the extreme radical and reactionary visions face new circumstances, requiring adjustments and reinterpretations. Within weeks of claiming a broad mandate for his agenda from the 2004 election, George W. Bush found his Republican caucus in Congress split on major priorities, with factions battling for control of the agenda. We believe these three forces are presently emerging in ways that create conditions for the reemergence of a left-leaning middle, animated by an expanded radical vision.

REDEFINING THE TERMS OF THE DEBATE

The polarities that dominated the late twentieth century, while still important in the present, are resolving and drifting to a settled past. Meanwhile, new polarities are developing to create the contours of the struggles of the near future. These new polarities can be seen in the destabilization of key terms that rest in the heart of the visions of both the radical left and reactionary right. As these terms become stretched and stolen, the contradictions embedded in them become the touchstones for discussing what we believe will be the new polarities for defining the future.

The key terms propelling the redefinition of the reactionary and radical visions are *nation*, *community*, and *sacred*. We will discuss the tensions and contradictions clustering around these terms and how each is introducing new polarities into public deliberations: the global-local conflict, individual advancement versus a sense of community and common purpose, and religious fundamentalism versus inclusive spirituality. The evolving polarizations around these key terms are fracturing both political extremes, but in very different ways. For the radical left, the interplay of these tensions offers a potential to enrich and expand the liberal-left vision. These same trends and terms are having the opposite effect on the reactionary vision, raising contradictions that undermine and erode its cohesion and unity.

Although the right wing dominates public discussion at the moment, it does so in the larger context of the acceptance by the vast majority of Americans of major elements of the radical perspective. As we look into the future, we see that the political middle will begin its realignment to new circumstances with a leftward lean. This liberal-left tilt is accentuated by two factors: the reactionary vision is being stretched and pulled apart by emerging divisions within the perspective, and it is increasingly finding it difficult to provide a coherent, unified perspective on key issues emerging as society wrestles with the deeper paradigm shift toward poetic humanism. This mounting tension soon will be compounded by the newly invigorated liberal vision that resonates much more fully with the paradigm shift on concepts of community, spirituality, and equality.

Global/Local Tensions: Contradictions in Nationalism

The concept and role of the nation-state is complex. Until recent times, however, it has been a fairly stable term in the visions of both the right and the left, representing a secure place in the political views of the middle. Recently, as global economic and political relationships have evolved, this stable concept has become contested. Disagreements over the role of international organizations, alliances, trade agreements, and the use of military force to secure national interests are intensifying.

For the political right, tensions between national and global interests are dividing an earlier coalition. For most of its history, the right has been associated with an intense nationalism flowing from its vision of the United States as a nation blessed and chosen by God. This nationalistic perspective and its advocacy of all things American is colliding head-on with the drive to participate in a global economy.

Economic tensions are connected to a reinterpretation of God's purpose. In the earlier right vision, America had a special purpose, what Ronald Reagan liked to call the "shining city on the hill." America was chosen by God to serve as a beacon to humankind.[36] However, that special purpose is now being challenged. In the most reactionary circles, God's purpose is no longer attached to a special view of America, but to a view of the present moment as one approaching Armageddon, or the final contest between good and evil. Among elements in the reactionary end of the spectrum, the present is cast as the time when the prophecies of last days are being fulfilled in preparation for the final coming of Christ to rule the world. In this scenario, national interest is important only in so far as it moves the world closer to the final days.[37]

Over the last two decades, varying economic interests and interpretations of God's purpose have complicated the role of the nation-state. Such complications are forcing realignment within the right on the emerging polarity between global interests and local concerns. Since the early 1980s, Republican elites, with the help of some Democrats, have been moving toward greater participation in the global economy and encouraging the development of trade alliances and institutions to support the activities. This emphasis on globalization is often over the opposition of their base constituencies. In the reactionary right, prominent representatives like Jerry Falwell reject such efforts at global economic interdependence. Falwell opposed the establishment of a North American Free Trade Agreement (NAFTA), for example, while most on the right supported it.[38]

Nation is no longer a stable term. Long a symbol that undergirded the patriotism of the right-conservative vision, the term now invokes differing visions that suggest different policy alternatives. This is evident in the differences emerging over the use of military power to protect American interests. The invasion and occupation of Iraq are supported by those of the Armageddon perspective and contested by those holding to the earlier reactionary vision. Both Pat Robertson and William F. Buckley Jr., who embrace the vision of the United States as the "shining city," reject the American actions in Iraq. While criticism was muted to assist in the election of George W. Bush in 2004, the votes were barely counted before the splits in this united front began to reopen.[39]

Thus the cohesion of purpose provided by a stable understanding of the key term *nation* is coming apart. The special role of the United States is being deemphasized as the millennial visions of Armageddon vie with earlier biblical interpretations of America's special purpose. As a result, the extreme right-wing base finds itself conflicted as global trade and military expansion take center stage in national deliberations. The nationalism versus global expansion dilemma fractures a core element of the right-wing vision and over time diminishes its hold on the center.

This dichotomy of nationalism and global expansion is also having an impact on stable visions of the extreme left. But rather than diminishing the radical vision, the pull for global justice is enriching and expanding the sphere of political activity. The demand for equality is extending beyond national borders to include a greater sense of global economic justice. The enlarged radical vision advocates equitable and sustainable development, multilateral peaceful cooperation among nations, and limitations on the accumulation and use of wealth at the expense of communities. It builds on the long radical tradition in the United States. The key term *nation* is deepened rather than divided. Placing itself in opposition to global corporations, the extreme left is able to embrace global connections through the extension of concepts of justice and sustainable development. Likewise it is able to position local control and national action within a framework of enriching democracy and democratic processes. Thus for the radical left, the global-local tension strengthens and enlarges its vision.

The rhetorical strategies of the left, however, remain consistent with earlier radicals. Emphasizing agency, the new radicals look at global structures of capital and decision making to argue for change. Wendell Berry places the new vision within the context of the war on terrorism:

I. The time will soon come when we will not be able to remember the horrors of September 11 without remembering also the unquestioning technological and economic optimism that ended on that day.

II. This optimism rested on the proposition that we were living in a new "world order" and a "new economy" that would "grow" on and on, bringing a prosperity of which every new increment would be "unprecedented."

III. The dominant politicians, corporate officers, and investors who believed this proposition did not acknowledge that the prosperity was limited to a tiny percent of the world's people, . . . and that its ecological costs increasingly threatened all life. . . .

IV. There was, as a consequence, a growing worldwide counter-effort on behalf of economic decentralization, economic justice, and ecological responsibly. We must recognize that the events of September 11 make this effort more necessary than ever.[40]

In the decade ahead, the emerging contours of this radical movement are pulling political positions leftward toward greater equality. The most extreme radical left, currently exemplified by the anarchist anti-corporate-globalization movement, emphasizes the need for new structures of society rooted in local concerns, emphasizing local control and sustainable development.

Liberals, too, are drawn toward acceptance of the expanding radical vision, but they remain committed to the current structures for achieving them. After a year of mass mobilizations against them, for example, liberal leaders of the WTO began to talk about greater economic equality, while emphasizing the need to maintain global structures.[41]

Community and the Common Good

Invoked by the image of the global, its opposite is the image of the local. The image of the local is expressed in an emerging discourse on *community*, of life lived in connection with others and with place. The concern for the protection and creation of community is also emerging to redefine political alignments.

For the radical left, the idea of economic and social justice allows the boundaries of community to expand. Terms invoking the idea of a global community or family of nations inform a radical view of a future made up of vibrant, self-sustaining, ecologically sensitive, locally based, and globally conscious associations. In this view, for the left of center, government is envisioned as an active, participatory democracy, where the people closest to the consequences of the decisions have the power to make them. This view of community is expressed in the radical slogan "think globally, and act locally."

The right-of-center conservatives have no such future vision to offer those seeking connection and community. Rather, their vision rests on associations from the past. They often describe the community for which they are striving as one now lost. They refer to earlier times when everyone knew their place, where life was well ordered and decisions were clearly based on principle. In the vision of the right, it is the loss of community that compels action, not the desire to create it anew. For those with a conservative orientation, the emphasis on the individual only highlights the absence of community. For the reactionary, a call to grand purpose provides little room for envisioning complex association.

At the same time, as relationships between people become more fragile and as the experience of community erodes, people seek new ways of connecting with one another.[42] In recent years, successful radical-left activities like conversation cafes and political salons orchestrated through the Internet bear witness to the power of connection. As this longing for community deepens, the contradiction between the individual emphasis of right of center ideology and the desire for community will grow.

This will mean that the extreme right, where the individual ideology is softened by the experience of a faith community, will not be able to translate concern for common responsibilities into policy initiatives to animate conservatives or attract the middle. As the far-right effort to privatize government services escalates, the increasing isolation from a sense of community life will intensify. Thus we should expect to see conservatives beginning to separate from reactionaries over the role of government in providing basic services like roads, schools, fire protection, hospitals, and other areas of common life. Conservatives are likely to look back to the earlier emphasis on small, efficient government and to find alliances with more radical efforts to protect local governments and communities.

On the left, the creation of sustainable, productive, and equitable community relationships is at the heart of their vision. Thus the longing of people for authentic relationships extends and deepens the capacity of the left to bring people together in a meaningful way. Starhawk, among the most active voices for the sense of community inspired by a sense of spirit, provides a glimpse of the radical view in her description of the anti-globalization struggle:

> We have knowledge and wisdom if we choose to apply them, about how to provide for human needs in ways that respect and enhance the balance of life. And we have a growing, global community of people committed to balanced ways of living. In this crucial time, we are called to be healers—of the earth, of the human community, of each other and ourselves.[43]

Science and the Sacred

The search for community and connection provides a foundation for the tensions around the third key term, *sacred*, and its implied polarity, science. The tensions around the sacred, however, are more than a simple dialectical tension between science and theology. Complicated by the paradigm shift from science to poetic humanism, the polar axis between science and spirituality is compounded by the polarity between a narrow religious fundamentalism and an expansive, inclusive spirituality.

The relationship between religion and politics has a complicated and often uneasy history in the United States.[44] On the one hand, religious beliefs and spiritual sensibilities have fueled some important left of center, liberal efforts to achieve justice, just as they have provided the source of right and reactionary sense of purpose. Religion has been used to justify liberation and repression. The abolitionist movement, civil rights movement, and the long history of pacifism in the United States all share deep religious roots. Likewise, the Judeo-Christian's foundational belief that God has a divine order for the world is integral to the right's vision. The idea that the United States is a chosen nation has a deeply Christian base. Such darker moments of our history as slavery, a restricted role for women, and attacks on indigenous people have all been justified by interpretations of religious doctrine. Whether from the right or left, religious revivals have historically preceded great social changes and accelerated the drift toward equality.[45]

Religion, characterized by Burke as an orientation predating science, influences current understanding of the right as it addresses new and complicated questions raised by advances in science. The center-right conservative has a long, uneasy relationship with science. Drawing on a literal interpretation of the Bible, people identifying as right of center have often opposed Darwinian theories of evolution as well as theories of the origin of the universe. Creationism and the so-called intelligent design theory offer pseudosciences based more in religious faith than scientific method. More recently, some have drawn on religious notions of the sanctity of life as the basis for opposing reproductive technologies, abortion, contraception, and stem-cell research.

Placing an emphasis on faith over science, the right-wing elements of the Republican Party galvanized conservative-reactionary voters. However, this emphasis also revealed tensions inherent in the decision to place principles of faith above science. This was especially evident during the 2004 election campaign and the issue of stem-cell research. Nancy Reagan and her son Ron openly opposed the Republican Party platform limiting stem-cell research, even as the party claimed itself heirs of the Reagan revolution.[46]

For many on the extreme right, a literal, fundamentalist interpretation of the Bible provides the outlines of the reactionary social agenda. Three aspects figure prominently in a vision for change: restoration of men to the head of the household, the public honoring of Christian values and prayer, and the protection of marriage from same-sex relationships. They not only reject the drift toward the secular and more equal world, but also reject the institutional supports for this drift, arguing that the Constitution has been perverted by activist courts influenced by liberals. Thus they seek to overturn the legal framework that supports a bright line between church and state, rejecting both the drift and structure of the society.

The implications of this fundamentalist belief are not shared by many in the conservative, center-right arena who join with their left of center and liberal counterparts in a firm commitment to the separation of church and state and a broader vision of social tolerance. By accepting the basic structures dividing church and state, the conservative position separates from the reactionary right. Thus while the extreme expression of faith over science may energize a base constituency, it alienates and marginalizes the reactionary right from the more conservative and moderate Republican middle. The reactionary advocates a view of the United States as a Christian nation in which Christian principles should govern public life. Conservatives agreeing with much of the tenor of this view hold for a more inclusive view of religious tolerance.[47]

While the right can be characterized as struggling to reconcile faith with science, the left is engaging in a reevaluation of this relationship. Once considered the epitome of reason and objectivity, center-left liberals are posing critical questions about the preeminent role given to science. Under pressures from the more radical left, some are beginning to question the positioning of scientific observation and analysis as the primary source of knowledge. In the more radical area, science is seen as only one of many ways of knowing. This expanded view of science has emerged in New Age spiritual practices, new physics, paganism, eco-feminism, and radical religious actions. For example, Starhawk, writing as a witch and eco-feminist, contrasts the compartmentalized mechanistic, cause-effect model of science with magic:

> Magic is, in a sense pattern-thinking. The world is not a mechanism made up of separate parts, but a whole made up of smaller wholes. In a whole, everything is interconnected and interactive and reflective of the whole. . . . When science and spirit are reconciled, the world becomes re-enchanted, full of wonder and magic. The great conversation is happening around us in many dimensions. Magic might also be called the art of opening our awareness to the consciousnesses that surround us, the art of conversing in the deep language that nature speaks.[48]

Like the debate over global-local relationships, this area promises to invigorate the left-center.

CONCLUSION

In the coming period, the roles of science, religion, and the sacred are forcing a new discourse. Tomorrow, we will see conservatives and liberals addressing spiritual concerns and spiritual needs. We will see people addressing the suffering and violence in the world with reasoned dialogue enriched with an understanding of political ideology and the images of a deep, shared context. Tomorrow, conservatives and liberals will be talking about the bottom line not only economically but spiritually.

Democracy is a living concept, evolving, growing, dying, and regenerating. Political ideology connects us in the present to the vision of the past we honor and the future we hope to achieve. In the coming years, as political discourse reconnects with ideology, we believe the United States will move toward a new vision of a just society where people live in harmony with one another and with the earth that supports our life. As Americans engage one another to determine the direction of the nation toward greater social control or greater equality, the broad consensus governing the political middle will again reassert itself. This assertion invites a new discourse on issues of community, ways of knowing, the mutual respect among nations, and spirituality. Another world is constantly in the making.

NOTES

1. Mark E. Huglen, "An Image of Online Education as 'Poetic Humanism,' " *Kentucky Journal of Communication* 23 (2004): 43–54.

2. Kenneth Burke, *Permanence and Change: An Anatomy of Purpose*, 3rd ed. (1935; Berkeley: University of California Press, 1984), 59–66.

3. Karl Polanyi, *The Great Transformation: The Political and Economic Origins of Our Time* (Boston: Beacon Press, 1952).

4. Immanual Wallerstein, "A Primer on U.S. Presidential Elections," Commentary No. 142, August 1, 2004, Fernand Braudel Center, Binghamton University, http://fbc.binghamton.edu/commentr.htm (August 16, 2004).

5. Immanual Wallerstein, "Quo Vadis America?" Commentary No. 141, July 15, 2004, Fernand Braudel Center, Binghamton University, http://fbc.binghamton.edu/commentr.htm (July 17, 2004).

6. Kevin Phillips, *Wealth and Democracy: A Political History of the American Rich* (New York: Random House, 2002), 405–6.

7. Paul Ray and Sherry Anderson, *The Cultural Creatives: How 50 Million People Are Changing the World* (New York: Harmony, 2001).

8. Howard Zinn, "The Optimism of Uncertainty," *Nation*, September 20, 2004, www.thenation.com/doc.mhtml?I=20040920=zinn (November 7, 2004).

9. Vincent Harding, *Hope and History: Why We Must Share the Story of the Movement* (Maryknoll, N.Y.: Orbis Books, 1990).

10. Zinn, "The Optimism of Uncertainty."

11. Richard Hofstader, *The American Political Tradition* (New York: Vintage Books, 1948), x.

12. Gunnar Myrdal, *An American Dilemma: The Negro Problem and Modern Democracy* (New York: Pantheon, 1944), 4.

13. David Reinhard, *The Republican Right since 1945* (Lexington: University of Kentucky Press, 1983), 222.

14. Phillips, *Wealth and Democracy*, 405–22.

15. Arthur M. Schlesinger Jr., *The Cycles of American History* (Boston: Houghton Mifflin, 1986).

16. Schlesinger, *The Cycles of American History*, 23–25.

17. Schlesinger, *The Cycles of American History*, 24.

18. Schlesinger, *The Cycles of American History*, 27.

19. Wallerstein, "Quo Vadis America?"

20. Phillips, *Wealth and Democracy*, 388.

21. Kofi Annan, "We the Peoples," Millennium Report of the Secretary General of the United Nations, 2000, www.un.org/millennium/sg/report (September 15, 2004).

22. M. Kaldor, H. Anheier, and M. Glasius, eds., *Global Civil Society Yearbook 2003* (London: Centre for Civil Society and Centre for the Study of Global Governance, London School of Economics, 2003).

23. Naomi Klein, "Ditch the Distraction in Chief," *Nation*, July 29, 2004, www.thenation.com/doc.mhtml?i=20040816&s=klein (August 10, 2004).

24. Bill Moyers, "Battlefield Earth," AlterNet, www.alternet.org/story/20666 (December 8, 2004).

25. Faud Shaban, "11 September and the Millennialist Discourse: An Order of Words?" *Arab Studies Quarterly* 25 (2003).

26. Cliff Schecter, "Extremely Motivated: The Republican Party's March to the Right," *Fordham Urban Law Journal* 29 (2002).

27. Todd S. Purdum, "An Electoral Affirmation of Shared Values," *New York Times*, November 4, 2004, 1A, 6A.

28. Schecter, "Extremely Motivated."

29. David Brooks, "The Ruling Class War," *New York Times*, September 11, 2004, 31A.

30. Arnold Schwarzenegger, "The American Dream: Preserving the Dream," *Vital Speeches of the Day* 70, no. 23 (September 15, 2004): 722.

31. Robert Reich, *Tales of a New America: The Anxious Liberal's Guide to the Future* (New York: Vintage Books, 1988).

32. Barbara L. Graham, "Explaining Supreme Court Policymaking in Civil Rights: The Influence of the Solicitor General, 1953–2002," *Policy Studies Journal* 31 (2003).

33. Schwarzenegger, "The American Dream," 722.

34. Burke, *Permanence and Change*.

35. Schlesinger, *The Cycles of American History*.

36. David W. Houck and Amous Kiewe, *Actor, Ideologue, Politician: The Public Speeches of Ronald Reagan* (Westport, Conn.: Greenwood Press, 1993), 327.

37. Nicholas D. Kristof, "Apocalypse (Almost) Now," *New York Times*, November 24, 2004, 27(A).

38. Schecter, "Extremely Motivated."

39. Lou Cannon, "Can Bush Break the Second Term Jinx?" *New York Times*, November 9, 2004, 23A.

40. Wendell Berry, "Thoughts in the Presence of Fear," Orion Society, 2001, www.oriononline.org/pages/oo/sidebars/America/Berry.html (August 15, 2004).

41. Mike Moore, "Statement by Mike Moore at President Bill Clinton's Lunch, WTO's Seattle Ministerial Conference" (1999), www.wto.org/english/news_e/spmm_e/spmm17_e.htm (December 21, 2004).

42. Robert Putnam, *Bowling Alone: The Collapse and Revival of American Community* (New York: Simon and Schuster, 2000).

43. Starhawk, *The Earth Path: Grounding Your Spirit in the Rhythms of Nature* (New York: HarperCollins, 2004), 216.

44. Howard Zinn, "The Optimism of Uncertainty," *Nation*, September 2, 2004, www.thenation.com/doc.mhtml?i=20040920&s=zinn (September 9, 2004).

45. Phillips, *Wealth and Democracy*.

46. Randy Kennedy, "First Lady Defends Limits on Stem Cell Research," *New York Times*, August 10, 2004, 16A.

47. Amy Elizabeth Ansell, *Unraveling the Right: The New Conservatism in American Thought and Politics* (Boulder, Colo.: Westview Press, 1998), 167–68.

48. Starhawk, *The Earth Path*, 11–12.

Bibliography

Adams, Ian. *The Logic of Political Belief: A Philosophical Analysis of Ideology*. Savage, Md.: Barnes and Noble Books, 1989.

Adams, William C., ed. *Television Coverage of the 1980 Presidential Campaign*. Norwood, N.J.: Ablex, 1983.

"Afghanistan: Still No Peace." Canadian Broadcasting Corporation (September 24, 2004). www.cbc.ca/news/features/afghanistan_sagacontinues.html (December 15, 2004).

Annan, Kofi. "We the Peoples," UN Millenium speech before the United Nations, 2000 (September 15, 2004).

Ansell, Amy Elizabeth. *Unraveling the Right: The New Conservatism in American Thought and Politics*. Boulder, Colo.: Westview Press, 1998.

Aune, James Arnt. *Rhetoric and Marxism*. Boulder, Colo.: Westview Press, 1994.

Ayers, Michael. *Locke: Ideas and Things*. New York: Routledge, 1999.

Barth, Hans. *Truth and Ideology*. Trans. Frederic Lilge. Berkeley: University of California Press, 1976.

Beinart, Peter. "TRB from Washington: Quiet Time." *New Republic*, May 13, 2002.

Bell, Daniel. *The End of Ideology: On the Exhaustion of Political Ideas in the Fifties*. Glencoe, Ill.: Free Press, 1960.

Bennett, W. Lance. "The Ritualistic and Pragmatic Bases of Political Campaign Discourse." *Quarterly Journal of Speech* 63 (1977): 219–38.

Berry, Wendell. "Thoughts in the Presence of Fear." Orion Society, 2001. www.orion online.org/pages/oo/sidebars/America/Berry.html (August 15, 2004).

Binder, Sarah, Thomas Mann, Alan Murphy, and Paul Sahre. "Where Do They Stand?" *New York Times*, July 26, 2004.

Bitzer, Lloyd F. "The Rhetorical Situation." *Philosophy and Rhetoric* 1 (1968): 1–14.

Bork, Robert. *Slouching toward Gomorrah*. 2nd ed. New York: Regan Books, 1997.

Brock, Bernard L. "A Definition of Four Political Positions and a Description of Their Rhetorical Characteristics." Ph.D. diss., Northwestern University, 1965.

———. "Political Speaking: A Burkean Approach." *Critical Responses to Kenneth Burke*. Ed. William H. Rueckert. Minneapolis: University of Minnesota Press, 1966.

Brooks, David. "The Ruling Class War." *New York Times*, September 11, 2004.

Burke, Edmund. "An Extract from Speech at Bristol Previous to the Election." *Selected Prose of Edmund Burke* (1780). Ed. Sir Philip Magnus. www.ourcivilisation.com/smartboard/shop/burkee/extracts/chap8.htm (September 24, 2004).

Burke, Kenneth. *Attitudes toward History.* 3rd ed. 1937. Berkeley: University of California Press, 1984.

———. *A Grammar of Motives.* 1945. Berkeley: University of California Press, 1969.

———. *Permanence and Change: An Anatomy of Purpose.* 3rd ed. 1935. Berkeley: University of California Press, 1984.

———. *Philosophy of Literary Form.* 3rd ed. 1941. Berkeley: University of California Press, 1973.

———. *A Rhetoric of Motives.* 1950. Berkeley: University of California Press, 1969.

———. *The Rhetoric of Religion: Studies in Logology.* Boston: Beacon Press, 1961.

Bush, George H. W. "1988 Republican National Convention Acceptance Address," August 18, 1988. Republican National Convention, New Orleans, www.americanrhetoric.com/speeches/georgehbush1988rnc.htm (September 24, 2004).

Bush, George W. "Acceptance Speech," Republican National Convention, Philadelphia, August 3, 2000. www.2000gop.com/convention/speech/speech/speechbush.html (January 9, 2005).

———. "The Second Gore-Bush Presidential Debate," October 11, 2000. www.debates.org/pages/trans2000b.html (September 24, 2004).

———. "Remarks by the President after Two Planes Crash into World Trade Center," September 11, 2001. www.whitehouse.gov/news/releases/2001/09/20010911.html (September 4, 2004).

——— "Today We've Had a National Tragedy." Remarks at Emma Booker Elementary School, Sarasota, Fla., September 11, 2001. www.americanrhetoric.com/speeches/gwbush911florida.htm (November 28, 2004).

———. "Freedom Itself Was Attacked This Morning." Barksdale Air Force Base, La., September 11, 2001. www.americanrhetoric.com/speeches/gwbush911barksdale.htm (November 28, 2004).

———. "President Bush Addresses Congress and the Nation," September 20, 2001. www.whitehouse.gov/news/releases/2001/09/20010920-8.html (June 15, 2004).

———. "President Delivers State of the Union," January 28, 2002. www.whitehouse.gov/news/releases/2003/01/20030128-19.html (January 7, 2005).

———. "President's Remarks to the United Nations General Assembly," September 12, 2002. www.whitehouse.gov/news/releases/2002/09/20020912-1.html (September 24, 2004).

———. "President Speaks at 30th Annual March for Life on the Mall," January 22, 2003. www.whitehouse.gov/news/releases/2003/01/20030122-3.html (January 27, 2003).

———. "A Quality Teacher in Every Classroom: Improving Teacher Quality and Enhancing the Profession," January 28, 2003. www.whitehouse.gov/infocus/education/teachers/quality_teachers.html (December 5, 2004).

———. "State of the Union Address," January 20, 2004. www.whitehouse.gov/news/releases/2004/01/20040120-7.html (January 9, 2004).

———. "President Bush Addresses the Nation in Prime Time Press Conference," April 13, 2004. www.whitehouse.gov/news/releases/2004/04/20040413-20.html (September 24, 2004).

———. "2004 Republican National Convention Address," September 2, 2004. www.americanrhetoric.com/speeches/convention2004/georgewbushrnc.htm (September 24, 2004).

———. "The First Bush-Kerry Presidential Debate," September 30, 2004. www.debates.org/pages/trans2004a.html (January 3, 2005).

"Bush Leads Country on Spending Spree." *Detroit News*. December 28, 2003.

Cannon, Lou. "Can Bush Break the Second Term Jinx?" *New York Times*, November 9, 2004.

Capella, Joseph N., and Kathleen Hall Jamieson. *Spiral of Cynicism: The Press and the Public Good.* New York: Oxford University Press, 1997.

Center for Political Studies. *National Election Studies*, 1995–2000. University of Michigan, Ann Arbor. www.umich.edu/~nes (December 15, 2004).

Clinton, William J. "Address of the President to the Joint Session of Congress," September 22, 1993. www.ibiblio.org/nhs/supporting/remarks-final.html (January 7, 2005).

———. "State of the Union Address," January 19, 1999. www.cnn.com/ALLPOLITICS/stories/1999/01/19/sotu.transcript/ (January 8, 2005).

"Comments and Images of the World's Leaders Following September 11, 2001, Terrorist Attacks." September 11 News.com. International Reaction. www.september11news.com/InternationalReaction.htm (January 15, 2005).

Dotson, Betsy. "President Clinton Submits FY 2001 Budget." *Government Finance Review* 16 (April 2000): 2, 55.

Eagleton, Terry. *Ideology: An Introduction.* London: Verso, 1991.

———. *Marx.* New York: Routledge, 1999.

Falwell, Jerry, and Pat Robertson. Partial Transcript of Comments from *700 Club.* Beliefnet.com, September 13, 2001. www.beliefnet.com/story/87/story_8770_1.html (January 3, 2005).

Feinstein, Dianne. "Should the Senate Pass S.139, the Climate Stewardship Act?" *Congressional Digest* 83, no. 1 (2004): 1617.

Ford, James E., and James F. Klumpp. "Systematic Pluralism: An Inquiry into the Bases of Communication Research." *Critical Studies in Mass Communication* 2 (1985): 408–29.

Frank, Thomas. "Why They Won." *New York Times*, November 5, 2004.

Gaus, Gerald F. *Justificatory Liberalism: An Essay on Epistemology and Political Theory.* New York: Oxford University Press, 1996.

Gaus, Gerald F., and Shane D. Courtland. "Liberalism." *The Stanford Encyclopedia of Philosophy.* Winter 2003 ed. Ed. Edward N. Zalta. http://plato.stanford.edu/archives/win2003/entries/liberalism/ (January 8, 2005).

Goodstein, Laurie, and William Yardley. "President Benefits from Effort to Build a Coalition of Religious Voters." *New York Times*, November 5, 2004.

Graham, Barbara L. "Explaining Supreme Court Policymaking in Civil Rights: The Influence of the Solicitor General, 1953–2002." *Policy Studies Journal* 31 (2003): 253–71.

Gramsci, Antonio. *Selections from the Prison Notebooks of Antonio Gramsci*. Ed. and trans. Quintin Hoare and Geoffrey Nowell Smith. New York: International Publishers, 1972.

Hagel, Chuck. "Should the Senate Pass S.139, the Climate Stewardship Act?" *Congressional Digest* 83, no. 1 (2004): 13–16.

Harding, Vincent. *Hope and History: Why We Must Share the Story of the Movement*. Maryknoll, N.Y.: Orbis Books, 1990.

Hertsgaard, Mark. "A New Ice Age?" *Nation*, March 1, 2004, 7–8.

Hobbes, Thomas. *Leviathan*. Ed. Michael Oakeshott. Oxford: Blackwell, 1948.

Hofstader, Richard. *The American Political Tradition*. New York: Vintage Books, 1948.

Houck, David W., and Amous Kiewe. *Actor, Ideologue, Politician: The Public Speeches of Ronald Reagan*. Westport, Conn.: Greenwood Press, 1993.

Huglen, Mark E. "An Image of Online Education as 'Poetic Humanism.'" *Kentucky Journal of Communication* 23 (2004): 43–54.

Huglen, Mark E., and Basil B. Clark. *Poetic Healing: A Vietnam Veteran's Journey from a Communication Perspective*. Revised and expanded ed. West Lafayette, Ind.: Parlor Press, 2005.

"Iraq War Illegal, Says Annan," British Broadcasting Service (September 16, 2004), http://news.bbc.co.uk/2/hi/middle_east/3661134.stm (September 24, 2004).

Jamieson, Kathleen Hall, and Paul Waldman, *The Press Effect: Politicians, Journalists and the Stories That Shape the Political World*. New York: Oxford, 2003.

Johnson, Haynes, and David S. Broder. *The System: The American Way of Politics at the Breaking Point*. Boston: Little, Brown, 1996.

Kaldor, M., H. Anheier, and M. Glasius, eds. *Global Civil Society Yearbook 2003*. London: Centre for Civil Society and Centre for the Study of Global Governance, London School of Economics, 2003.

Kennedy, Randy. "First Lady Defends Limits on Stem Cell Research." *New York Times*, August 10, 2004.

Kerry, John. "Speech to the 2004 Democratic National Convention," July 29, 2004. www.johnkerry.com/pressroom/speeches/spc_2004_0729.html (September 24, 2004).

Klein, Naomi. "Ditch the Distraction in Chief." *Nation*, July 29, 2004.

Klumpp, James, Daniel Sullivan, and Dennis Garrett. "The Issue-Image Dichotomy: A Study of Political Communication and TV News." Paper presented at the Central States Speech Association Convention, Detroit, Mich., April 1977.

Klumpp, James F., and Thomas A. Hollihan. "Debunking the Resignation of Earl Butz: Sacrificing an Official Racist." *Quarterly Journal of Speech* 65 (1979): 1–11.

Krane, David K. *Harris Poll*, No. 47 (June 30, 2004).

Kristof, Nicholas D. "Apocalypse (Almost) Now," *New York Times*, November 24, 2004.

Leibovich, Mark, and Jim VandeHei. "New Blood at Heart of Kerry Campaign: Some See Changes as a Last Chance." *Washington Post*, September 17, 2004.

Lerner, Michael. "Democrats Need a Spiritual Left." *Common Dreams*.org (November 4, 2004). www.commondreams.org (November 5, 2004).

Lichtheim, George. "The Concept of Ideology." *History and Theory* 4 (1964–1965): 164–95.

Madison, James. *The Federalist Papers*, No. 10.

Mannheim, Karl. *Ideology and Utopia*. Trans. Louis Wirth and Edward Shils. 1929. New York: Harcourt, Brace, and World, 1966.

Martire, Ralph. Editorial. *Chicago Sun-Times*, October 9, 2004.

Marx, Karl, and Friedrich Engels. *The German Ideology*.

McCain, John. "Should the Senate Pass S.139, the Climate Stewardship Act?" *Congressional Digest* 83, no. 1 (2004): 12–13.

McGee, Michael Calvin. "The 'Ideograph': A Link between Rhetoric and Ideology." *Quarterly Journal of Speech* 66 (1980): 1–16.

Mill, John Stuart. *Utilitarianism and Other Essays*. Ed. Alan Ryan. New York: Viking, 1987.

Moore, Mike. "Statement by Mike Moore at President Bill Clinton's Lunch." WTO's Seattle Ministerial Conference, 1999. www.wto.org/english/news_ e/spmm_e/spmm17_e.htm (December 21, 2004).

Morin, Richard, and Claudia Deane. "Bush Has Wide Support in Crisis, Poll Shows," *Washington Post*, September 23, 2001.

———. "In Poll, Americans Back Bush." *Washington Post*, November 8, 2001.

Moyers, Bill. "Battlefield Earth." AlterNet.org. www.alternet.org/story/20666 (December 8, 2004).

Myrdal, Gunnar. *An American Dilemma: The Negro Problem and Modern Democracy*. New York: Pantheon, 1944.

Nader, Ralph. "Iraq War and Occupation." Nader/Camejo 2004. www.votenader.org/issues/index.php?cid=17 (January 8, 2005).

National Security Strategy of the United States. Washington: GPO, 2002. www.whitehouse.gov/nsc/nss.html (September 24, 2004).

"Network News Coverage of '04 Primaries Falls Short, Study Finds." Alliance for Better Campaigns: Political Standard, May 2004. www.ourairwaves.org/standard/display.php?StoryID=314 (November 24, 2004).

Newman, Bruce I. *The Mass Marketing of Politics: Democracy in an Age of Manufactured Images*. Thousand Oaks, Calif.: Sage, 1999.

Ogden, C. K., and I. A. Richards. *The Meaning of Meaning*. 8th ed. New York: Harcourt, Brace, 1946.

Patterson, Thomas E. *The Vanishing Voter: Public Involvement in an Age of Uncertainty*. New York: Knopf, 2002.

Patterson, Thomas E., and Robert D. McClure. *The Unseeing Eye: The Myth of Television Power in National Elections*. New York: Putnam, 1976.

Pepper, Stephen. *World Hypotheses*. Berkeley: University of California Press, 1942.

Phillips, Kevin. *Wealth and Democracy: A Political History of the American Rich*. New York: Random House, 2002.

Pincus, Walter, and Dana Milbank. "Al Qaeda–Hussein Link Is Dismissed." *Washington Post*, June 17, 2004.

Polanyi, Karl. *The Great Transformation: The Political and Economic Origins of Our Time*. Boston: Beacon Press, 1952.

Powell, Colin. "U.S. Secretary of State Colin Powell Addresses the U.N. Security Council." February 5, 2003. www.whitehouse.gov/news/releases/2003/02/20030205-1.html (September 24, 2004).

Priest, Dana. "Al Qaeda–Iraq Link Recanted: Captured Libyan Reverses Previous Statement to CIA Officials Say." *Washington Post*, August 1, 2004.

Purdum, Todd S. "An Electoral Affirmation of Shared Values." *New York Times*, November 4, 2004.

———. "A Steamroller That May Lose Its Steam. *New York Times*, November 28, 2004.

Putnam, Robert. *Bowling Alone: The Collapse and Revival of American Community*. New York: Simon and Schuster, 2000.

Ray, Paul, and Sherry Anderson. *The Cultural Creatives: How 50 Million People Are Changing the World*. New York: Harmony, 2001.

Reagan, Ronald. "State of the Union Address." January 25, 1984. www.usa-presidents.info/union/reagan-3.html (January 8, 2005).

Reich, Robert. *Tales of a New America: The Anxious Liberal's Guide to the Future*. New York: Vintage Books, 1988.

Reinhard, David. *The Republican Right since 1945*. Lexington: University of Kentucky Press, 1983.

Republican House Leaders. "Contract with America." 1994. www.house.gov/house/Contract/Contract.html (September 24, 2004).

Robinson, Michael J., and Margaret A. Sheehan. *Over the Wire and on TV: CBS and UPI in Campaign '80*. New York: Russell Sage Foundation, 1983.

Roosevelt, Franklin. "First Inaugural Address." March 4, 1933. www.americanrhetoric.com/speeches/fdrfirstinaugural.html (September 24, 2004).

Rorty, Richard. *Philosophy and Social Hope*. New York: Penguin Books, 1999.

Rossiter, Clinton. *Conservatism in America*. New York: Vintage Books, 1962.

Rothschild, Mathew. "Bush: I'm God's Delivery Boy." *Progressive*, March 16, 2004. www.progressive.org/webex04/wx031604.html (August 16, 1004).

Rushdie, Salmon. "America and Anti-Americans," *New York Times*, February 4, 2002.

Sandel, Michael J. "Easy Virtue." *New Republic*, September 2, 1996.

Schecter, Cliff. "Extremely Motivated: The Republican Party's March to the Right." *Fordham Urban Law Journal* 29 (2002): 1663.

Schlesinger, Arthur M., Jr. *The Cycles of American History*. Boston: Houghton Mifflin, 1986.

Schwarzenegger, Arnold. "The American Dream: Preserving the Dream," *Vital Speeches of the Day* 70, no. 23 (September 15, 2004): 720.

Schwartz, Tony. *The Responsive Chord*. Garden City, N.Y.: Anchor Books, 1972.

Shaban, Faud. "11 September and the Millennialist Discourse: An Order of Words?" *Arab Studies Quarterly* 25 (2003): 13–32.

Sontag, Susan. "Talk of the Town." *New Yorker*, September 24, 2001.

Sperling, John. *The Great Divide: Retro versus Metro America*. Sausalito, Calif.: Poli-Point Press, 2004.

Starhawk. *The Earth Path: Grounding Your Spirit in the Rhythms of Nature*. New York: HarperCollins, 2004.

"Student Prayer Case Reaches Supreme Court." *Techniques*, February 2000.

Suskind, Ron. *The Price of Loyalty: George W. Bush, the White House, and the Education of Paul O'Neill*. New York: Simon and Schuster, 2004.

Taylor, Jerry."Oh, No! That '70s Show: Against Carterism in Energy Policy" A Cato Commentary National Review. March 25, 2002. www.cato.org/research/articles/taylor-020325.html (January 17, 2005).

Teo Chu Cheow, Eric. "Anti-Americanism Rises in Asia." *Japan Times*, January 11, 2003.

Therborn, Goeran. *The Ideology of Power and the Power of Ideology*. London: Verso, 1980.

Toner, Robin. "Southern Democrats' Decline Is Eroding the Political Center." *New York Times*, November 15, 2004.

Toulmin, Stephen. *The Uses of Argument*. Cambridge: Cambridge University Press, 1958.

United States Census Bureau. *Voting and Registration in the Election of November 1996*. July 1998. www.census.gov/prod/3/98pubs/p20-504/pdf (September 26, 2004).

Wallerstein, Immanual. "A Primer on U.S. Presidential Elections." Commentary No. 142, August 1, 2004. Fernand Braudel Center, Binghamton University. http://fbc.binghamton.edu/commentr.htm (August 16, 2004).

———. "Quo Vadis America?" Commentary No. 141, July 15, 2004. Fernand Braudel Center, Binghamton University. http://fbc.binghamton.edu/commentr.htm (July 17, 2004).

Walsh, Kenneth T., and Kent Jenkins Jr. "The Deal of a Generation: A Five-year Plan to Get to a Balanced Budget." *U. S. News and World Report*, May 12, 1997.

Weaver, Richard. *The Ethics of Rhetoric*. South Bend, Ind.: Regnery/Gateway, 1953.

———. *Language Is Sermonic*. Ed. Richard L. Johannesen, Rennard Strickland, and Ralph T. Eubanks. Baton Rouge: Louisiana State University Press, 1970.

Williams, Raymond. *Marxism and Literature*. Oxford: Oxford University Press, 1977.

Zinn, Howard. "The Optimism of Uncertainty." *Nation*. September 20, 2004. www.thenation.com/doc.mhtml?I=20040920=zinn (November 7, 2004).

Index

About the Authors

Bernard L. Brock (Ph.D., Northwestern University) is professor emeritus of communication and codirector of the Center for Arts and Public Policy at Wayne State University, Detroit. He is coauthor of *Rhetorical Criticism: A Twentieth Century Perspective* and *Public Policy Decision-Making* and editor of *Kenneth Burke and Contemporary European Thought* and *Kenneth Burke and the 21st Century*. He has written over eighty journal articles, book chapters, and newspaper articles.

Mark E. Huglen (Ph.D., Wayne State University) teaches communication at the University of Minnesota, Crookston. His books include *Argument Strategies from Aristotle's Rhetoric* with Norman E. Clark and *Poetic Healing: A Vietnam Veteran's Journey from a Communication Perspective*, revised and expanded with Basil B. Clark. He has written numerous articles in rhetorical theory and criticism.

James F. Klumpp (Ph.D., University of Minnesota) is associate professor of communication at the University of Maryland. He is coeditor of *American Rhetorical Discourse* and editor of *Argument in a Time of Change*. He is the author of forty articles in rhetorical theory, rhetorical criticism, and political communication.

Sharon Howell (Ph.D., Wayne State University) is professor of communication and chair of the Department of Rhetoric, Communication, and Journalism at Oakland University, Rochester, Michigan. She has recently coauthored studies in group communication with Bernard Brock and is a community activist in Detroit.